Emotional
Intensity

in Gifted Students

Helping Kids Cope With Explosive Feelings

D0029924

Emotional Intensity
in Gifted Students

Helping Kids Cope With Explosive Feelings

by
Christine Fonseca

PRUFROCK PRESS INC.
WACO, TEXAS

Library of Congress Cataloging-in-Publication Data

Fonseca, Christine, 1966-
 Emotional intensity in gifted students : helping kids cope with explosive feelings / by Christine Fonseca.
   p. cm.
 Includes bibliographical references.
 ISBN 978-1-59363-490-2 (pbk.)
 1. Gifted children--Education. 2. Gifted children--Behavior modification. 3. Emotional problems of children--Treatment. I.
Title.
 LC3993.F56 2011
 371.95--dc22
                        2010031833

Copyright © 2011, Prufrock Press Inc.
Edited by Lacy Compton
Layout Design by Raquel Trevino
Cover Design by Marjorie Parker

ISBN-13: 978-1-59363-490-2

Prufrock Press Inc.
P.O. Box 8813
Waco, TX 76714-8813
Phone: (800) 998-2208
Fax: (800) 240-0333
http://www.prufrock.com

TABLE OF CONTENTS

ACKNOWLEDGEMENTS

There are a lot of people who helped take my crazy dream of teaching parents about gifted children and make it into a book. To start, none of this would have happened without my super agent, Krista Goering, who bravely took a chance on my dream and helped me see it through—I know I would never have finished this book without her dedication to the project. My amazing editor, Lacy Compton, gave me a million and one ideas that made the book better than I thought possible. The entire team at Prufrock Press made my first book an experience I want to repeat over and over again.

Writing is never a solitary sport. There are so many supporters who helped to keep me focused when things got hard. My agent-sis and dear friend, Michelle McLean, saw this project go from an idea to the finished book. She read for me, cried with me, and held me together when I wanted to quit—I owe you huge! My first writing bud, Elana Johnson, convinced me that an agent would make this crazy dream of mine come to life—thanks for that. Thanks also for keeping me sane through everything. You are definitely my oxygen! And Julie Butcher Fedynich—your real-life stories shaped so much of this book! Diana Damon-White and Andree Grey inspired the idea for this book through their loving participation in my workshops. The amazing group of GATE parents and GATE teachers in the Temecula Valley Unified School District shared their stories and enabled this dream to begin.

These acknowledgements wouldn't be complete without a special thanks to my family: Daryn Fonseca and Karol Fonseca, who fed my muse with great music; my parents, Paul and Judi Warren, who taught me to dream big; my more-than-a-sister-in-law, Debbie Hernandez, who reminded me to be true to myself; my husband, Dirck, whose support kept our family together every time I disappeared into the writing cave, and to my two precocious, gifted daughters, Erika and Fabiana—to whom this manuscript is dedicated. I love you guys a million, trillion percent!

INTRODUCTION

WHY THIS BOOK

Parenting is a difficult job. You aren't given a manual when you have a child and there's no survival guide to tell you what to do. Things complicate further if your child is lucky enough to be gifted. People tell you it'll be easy raising a bright child, leaving you frustrated when your child begins to act a little . . . intense.

Fortunately there are parenting books to help—too many parenting books.

Most of these books don't address the unique needs of gifted children. In fact, as you attempt the strategies typically found in them, things often get worse. You're left feeling angry with your own inability to execute the strategies that are *supposed* to work so well.

Frustrated and resentful, you turn to other family members, friends, and the school looking for help. But the same misguided assumptions about giftedness abound, leaving you feeling even more inadequate.

As the negative feelings build, your child increases the intensity of her behaviors, adding fuel to the fire. The result? A chaotic household with few resources available to help.

That's where this book comes in. Designed to provide support for the difficult job of parenting gifted children, *Emotional Intensity in Gifted Students: Helping Kids Cope With Explosive Feelings* provides the resource you need to not only understand why gifted children are so extreme in their behavior, but also learn specific strategies to teach your children how to live with their intensity. Presented in a readable and practical format, I use case studies and role-playing techniques to make the information come to life and provide you with the tools needed to make a positive lasting impact on your child.

This book addresses:

✦ the assumptions most people make about giftedness;

✦ the cognitive, social, and emotional characteristics of being gifted and the problems created by those attributes;

✦ the emotional development and the intense nature of gifted children;

✦ the specific problems most gifted children face and strategies parents and educators can use to teach children to how to cope;

✦ the unique issues faced by dually exceptional children, including those who are gifted and diagnosed with learning disabilities or mental illness;

✦ how to utilize coaching techniques that minimize the negative attributes of giftedness; and

✦ how to collaborate with schools and mental health professionals.

HOW TO USE THIS BOOK

Emotional Intensity in Gifted Students was designed to be a reference guide for parents and educators. After reading and understanding the first section of the book, parents and educators can rely on Parts II and III to provide specific strategies found to be highly effective in working with gifted children. Part II provides a detailed explanation of various strategies for use at home and at school, including checklists to refer back to in times of crisis and many tips for handling specific types of problems. Part III explains how to switch from authoritative parenting and teaching strategies to a more "coaching" oriented approach. Specific role-plays are given to further teach the use of the strategies within the model of coaching and provide a way to check your own techniques.

As you begin to implement these strategies, different problems may arise. The detailed Recommended Resources section at the end of the book provides additional resources for many of the areas discussed throughout the book. Several worksheets, checklists, and tip sheets also are provided to help you implement the strategies I suggest throughout the book.

I wish you much success in being the coach your children need as they progress through their years and embrace everything it means to be gifted. My wish is that this book will provide a source of comfort and connection when things become too intense.

A WORD TO EDUCATORS

Although this book is designed for parents, many of the strategies can be easily adopted for use in the classroom. Teaching gifted children can be every bit as difficult as raising them. The intensity of their thinking, while a delight in the academic context, can be difficult with regard to their emotional development. This book is designed to address that difficulty.

Look for the "Notes to the Teacher" sections throughout the book for specific advice and strategies that can be utilized with gifted children. By working in collaboration with each other, educators and parents can make positive and meaningful impact on the lives of our gifted children.

PART I

WHAT IT REALLY MEANS TO BE GIFTED

CHAPTER 1
ASSUMPTIONS ABOUT GIFTEDNESS

Your 10-year-old child is easy to raise—most days. The rest of the time she is a handful. A big handful. A bit of an enigma, she possesses qualities of being both highly intelligent and completely ignorant when it comes to the mundane. She can be funny and make everyone laugh while also being serious to the point of critical. Her empathy runs high, as she cries at commercials about global warming. Yet she criticizes her friends who don't hold her worldview and often insists to you that her way is always the better way.

Her grades in school are good. But, her teachers complain that she often is sloppy in her work, makes careless errors on the simplest of math problems, and misspells basic words. She often chooses the road less traveled in all aspects of her life, wondering why others don't see that it is—at least to her—the easier way. Often a joy to be around, your child's moods can swing from one extreme to the other. The unbalanced nature of these mood swings causes you to question her emotional stability—and your own.

If you had to summarize her in one word, you would call her intense.

Parenting your child often leaves you frustrated as you vacillate between feeling lucky to have such a great kid and cursed for having to deal with her emotions.

Is she crazy? Are you?

Neither is true. You've just stumbled into the emotional world of gifted children and the drama of parenting and teaching them.

Assumptions are common with gifted children. People often assume that raising a highly curious, bright child is an easy task—something parents should be happy about all of the time. These same people feel that bright children do not fall prey to many of the problems that other children encounter, including poor academic achievement, bullying, or risky behaviors.

Although it is true that there are many rewards to being the parent of a gifted child, believing that a gifted child will be easy to raise only negates the very real challenges inherent in parenting this population. Furthermore, the emotional roller coaster that can accompany giftedness makes parenting a true challenge.

Gifted children face school challenges, difficulties with peers, and problems with overall emotional development, similar to their nongifted counterparts. However, the nature of giftedness makes these issues significantly more intense. Parents of gifted children often are conflicted in their feelings regarding their children—ranging from delight and marvel related to children's creativity and intellectual prowess, to frustration regarding children's poor stress response, to powerlessness when parents feel inept in their own understanding of how to help this unique breed of children. Educators, too, often feel a sense of powerlessness as they try to help their gifted students maintain emotional balance and control in the classroom and with their friends.

GIFTED CHILDREN AND SCHOOL

One of the biggest assumptions made about gifted children involves academic achievement. People assume that these children require little to no discipline or encouragement with regard to learning in the school setting, believing giftedness is the same as being a high-achieving student (Webb, Gore, Amend, & DeVries, 2007). Furthermore, it is assumed that gifted children will always find an intrinsic way to learn—there is no need for specialized academic programs or teacher education in the field of giftedness. Unfortunately, these assumptions do not reflect an accurate understanding of the nature of giftedness.

Many gifted children do perform well in school, equating school performance with something as fundamental as breathing. They require little to no assistance from teachers or parents.

However, a growing number of these students share a different reality when it comes to traditional learning. They are frustrated by the mundane and repetitive processes found in many classrooms. Driven by boredom, they fall out of sync with school and withdraw from the learning environment. Unlike their high-achieving counterparts, they are not intrinsically motivated by good grades, having already decided that school has nothing of particular value to offer them.

If this pattern is allowed to continue, these gifted children soon will find themselves unable to get by on pure intellect. Having missed important information in class due to the lack of engagement in learning, they struggle—typically for the very first time. By this point, teachers may not see their gifted qualities at all, and often will believe that someone must have "made a mistake" about the gifted label. If they are recognized as being intelligent, teachers will assume that these underachieving gifted children are just being *lazy*. Seldom is the problem recognized as a mismatch between how gifted children learn and what the school so regularly asks them to do: repetitive and routine tasks.

The reality is, at least 5% of gifted children fail or drop out of school (Renzulli & Park, 2000). This is a statistic that should make educators and parents feel uncomfortable. Maybe even outraged. Closer attention needs to be paid to the unique needs of gifted students if we are going to improve student outcomes for this population. Educational strategies including acceleration, differentiation, and grouping are things that need to be explored in order to help meet the needs of gifted children and improve their emotional and behavior outcomes.

ANDREW

Andrew is a 12-year-old sixth grader. Having been identified as gifted in second grade, Andrew enjoyed his early childhood school experiences. In third grade, he earned average grades in all classes and indicated that learning was fun. At home, he typically amused himself by taking things apart—his electronic toys, his mother's old PDA, and a broken computer. He needed to understand why things worked the way they did. His early grade school teachers reported that he was a creative and talented student. His parents could not have been more proud.

As time went on and Andrew entered fifth grade, things began to change. The curriculum, no longer new and exciting, had settled into a mixture of routine and rote activities, punctuated with occasional opportunities for enrichment (which, in Andrew's mind, always meant more work). Andrew began to show disinterest in school, avoiding homework and no longer speaking about his day with excitement. His parents became concerned and went to the teacher for help. She suggested a "token economy" to assist with homework completion, rewarding him based on work completion. This helped for a short while, only to have the problem persist.

Andrew continued to withdraw from school, finding little to stimulate his mind. At home he no longer took apart the computer. Now he designed video games, filling any available time with trying to stump his friends with his new games.

Although he completed little to no work in school, Andrew's test scores continued to be high. The teacher reassured his parents that this was just a phase, promising that he would grow out of it eventually.

However, this was not the case. By sixth grade, things had taken a serious turn for the worse. Andrew, no longer in the habit of completing schoolwork, discovered that his intellect alone was not enough to maintain passing grades. He completed no homework, failed most of his tests, and rarely demonstrated interest in school. He still designed video games at home and won various online contests.

His parents were at a loss as to what to do. Turning to the school, they were again told that it was a homework issue; if he would only do more homework, he would be fine. His standardized scores from statewide assessments continued to demonstrate high potential, so the school felt the problem was nothing more than a matter of laziness and poor parental structure.

Although Andrew is fictional, drawn from a combination of many real cases, his story is one that exemplifies the typical challenges some gifted children and parents face in the school system. We will revisit Andrew throughout the book, as we learn more about the complex challenges facing gifted students with regard to school.

GIFTED CHILDREN AND THEIR PEERS

Another commonly held myth is that gifted children get along fine in the social aspects of their lives, having little problems with bullies or friendships in general. Sometimes the opposite is assumed—that all gifted children are "geeks" or "nerds" by nature. Such stereotypes minimize the nature of the problems faced by these children as they try to build friendships (Webb et al., 2007).

Many gifted children struggle greatly in the social areas of their lives, related in part to the intensity of their behaviors, as well as the unique aspects of their personalities, both of which will be covered in more detail in subsequent chapters. In general, gifted students have a tendency to appear arrogant and unconnected to their peers, often finding interest in things other than the typical interests of their peers. Social relationships often are negatively impacted by their tendency to lose interest with the day-to-day triviality that typifies most relationships during childhood. Instead, these children would prefer to focus on larger world problems, or things that are abstract and complex—most of which is not appealing to typical nongifted peers. The result is a combination of frustration and avoidance, neither of which move toward strong interpersonal relationships.

Peer relationships naturally change over the course of childhood, especially as children enter their middle school years. For gifted children, the process of change can be even more difficult, as the move toward fitting in with their typical peers takes on a life of its own. Unable to compete socially due to the uniqueness of their personalities, these children often will hide their giftedness, trying hard to fit in to a social structure that eludes them. They may try out for a sport that the "cool" kids like, or fail classes to fit in with a particular peer group. Sometimes these kids will avoid accolades given by the adults on campus by missing outside events that reward academic achievement or getting "sick" just before awards ceremonies.

For some gifted students the opposite may be true. Faced with the knowledge that they can never fit in with the popular crowd, and not necessarily wanting to, they take on the personae of *super nerd*, a label that allows them to be above and beyond odd. For this group, being unusual is the prime objective, often leading to significant bullying from other groups of children. When this happens, educators often are at a loss as to how to help. Instead of recognizing the problem as something related to the way in which gifted children interact with the world and teaching tolerance, they struggle with trying to either teach the gifted child to change or telling the parent the acts of bullying are just normal kid behavior. We've seen all too often the long-term impact of bullying on any child, let alone a population of children that process the world intensely by nature.

Whether a gifted child is trying to bend herself into a pretzel to fit in or aiming to emulate the label of "nerd," these children suffer in their relationships, often struggling to find their own safe haven among their peers. The lack of friendships can lead to sincere pain for both the child and the parent. Both parties are left trying to grapple with the problem, not really understanding why such social connections are so hard.

MEREDITH

Meredith is an 8-year-old gifted girl in third grade. She thinks of herself as outgoing and smart with many friends. However, when she invites friends over for play dates, very few come. She finds herself ostracized on the playground at times—especially when she becomes overwrought during a tetherball game or when she doesn't get her way at recess. Things come to a head one day when she comes home crying, saying that "all" of her friends are refusing to play with her. Concerned, her parents go to the school looking for help. They watch their daughter interact with her friends and quickly begin to understand a part of the problem, as they witness their daughter bossing everyone. They watch in horror as the child tells everyone how wrong they are, refuses to let anyone choose a game, and argues about various rules. When the other children try to tell her that she is not being nice, she immediately gets angry and accuses them of just being jealous of her.

Her parents are shocked. Their own daughter is acting like a brat. Frustrated, they go home and talk with her that night. She cries, stating that she wasn't doing anything wrong. She goes on to say that she doesn't mean to sound bossy and that she just wants friends. The parents' frustration continues long after the conversation ends, as they feel powerless to change the situation. They don't know how to help the other children see the wonderful qualities that Meredith typically demonstrates at home.

Meredith's story—far from unique—paints the picture of what can happen as gifted students begin to enter the social arena of school, as well as the pain that can occur when children are unable to find success in that setting.

GIFTED CHILDREN AND THEIR EMOTIONS

Existing myths regarding gifted children not only reflect school performance or peer interactions, but also emotional development. One of the more commonly held beliefs is that gifted children are more prone to anxiety and/or depression than other children. Furthermore, some people in the general population believe that there is little to do regarding the anxiety and depression, other than treat it through therapy and/or medication. The truth about gifted children is actually quite different. Recent research indicates that gifted children often are more resilient than their nongifted counterparts (Mueller, 2009). Furthermore, the depression and anxiety-like behaviors that seem to go hand in hand with many gifted children may not be a *disorder* as much as a natural aspect of the gifted child's personality. These children are more emotionally intense than their nongifted counterparts, resulting in a host of behaviors that simulate anxiety and depression, among other things (Sword, 2006b). The cause of the behavior, however, is substantively different—something often ignored by both the educational and mental health fields.

Gifted children do struggle with their emotional development overall, despite good long-term prognoses. Problems regarding the stability of mood, existential depression, and performance-based anxiety are typical with this population, but for different reasons than similar traits in other children. Gifted children behave in this way as a direct outpouring of the intensity that defines this population, as opposed to a dysfunctional aspect of personality that needs to be fixed. Although the latter responds well to treatment designed to "fix" the problem, the former does not, as it is a normal aspect of many gifted children's development. These children require interventions that stem from a thorough understanding of the emotional nature of giftedness and an understanding of the typical intensity inherent in gifted individuals.

Such interventions need to focus on coping strategies as opposed to changing traits that are inherently part of who they are.

EMILY

Emily, a 16-year-old gifted student, is a high achiever. She also considers herself a fraud. Faced with a definition of being bright and high achieving given by the adults in her life, Emily assumes that she should not have to work as hard as she does to maintain her grades. She watches her high-achieving friends and feels that "they" must be gifted, because "they" do not appear to be working nearly as hard as she is. She has to study diligently, stay up late, and work very hard to uphold the 4.3 GPA she insists on maintaining.

In addition to school, Emily plays the piano, swims competitively, and participates in journalism and political clubs. In an effort to complete her required courses and get a head start on college, Emily takes additional classes at the local college campus. She also tutors younger children to help supplement the funds required for her college education.

Emily is under a lot of stress. She deals with the stress in somewhat explosive ways, often melting down into a heap in her room. During these times, Emily will throw things and yell at anyone who asks her anything. This includes siblings and her parents, especially her parents. After her tirades, Emily will feel extreme remorse, causing her to sob and cry, sometimes for hours on end. When Emily looks back on her behavior, she believes that something is wrong with her—that she is somehow damaged or crazy.

Emily's parents are extremely frustrated with her. Her mood swings have raised havoc in the household, causing major disruptions in everyday routines. They feel there is something seriously wrong with her. Unsure of how to proceed, they discuss the problems with her school and their medical doctor, both of whom suggest counseling. The counselor, taking in the information provided by the parents, becomes concerned with anxiety, depression, and mood problems. A treatment plan involving significant amounts of medication, as well as therapy, is developed. Although Emily is happy to get help, she can't help believing that getting help means she really *is* crazy—very crazy, in her opinion.

Emily's story is not as simple as it may sound. The behavior certainly could point to mental health issues. However, the behavior taken out of the context of Emily's intellect does not paint a complete picture. The intensity of her emotions is extreme, and it does mimic a mood disorder. However, differentiating between a mood disorder and the normal intensity of behavior associated with giftedness and stress requires thoroughly understanding the giftedness in order to develop an appropriate treatment plan—something that is not always considered.

Overall, the many assumptions regarding the true nature of giftedness serve only to misrepresent the joys and problems of being gifted. True challenges in academic, social, and emotional arenas are overlooked and misunderstood, resulting in the negation of the difficulties really faced by teachers, parents, and children. The next few chapters will further explore the truth behind the characteristics of giftedness, and the impact of these characteristics on overall functioning.

NOTES TO THE TEACHER

The vast majority of assumptions and myths surrounding giftedness revolve around education. The Fall 2009 edition of *Gifted Child Quarterly (GCQ)* identified 19 popular myths related to giftedness (see Treffinger, 2009). These myths aren't new. In fact, a 1982 edition of the same publication originally identified many of these concerns in an editorial by Don Treffinger. And yet, despite advocacy, research, and the support of organizations like the National Association for Gifted Children (NAGC), the mythology continues. Worse, perpetuation of these myths and assumptions serves only to distort the true needs of gifted children and maintain the status quo in education.

Some of the assumptions unique to education include the belief that specific teaching strategies geared toward this population are not necessary because gifted children learn in all settings. Others include the belief that all children have the capacity for giftedness; therefore, as long as a teacher is challenging all students, no specific understanding of giftedness is necessary. Both of these myths negate the very real and unique aspects of giftedness related to personality and emotional attributes. Furthermore, they oversimplify the realities facing many teachers of gifted students who underachieve, placing blame on the student and parents instead of recognizing the need for collaboration between all parties in order to improve student outcomes.

One of the most common education-related assumptions is that acceleration is socially damaging to gifted children. Although grade skipping can have a negative impact on some gifted children, the research indicates that this is not true for all students (Kulik, 2004). It is important to be well grounded in an understanding of giftedness and the unique needs of the individual student when making educational placement decisions. This is particularly true in both cases of acceleration and in dealing with gifted students who are dually exceptional (these students also are sometimes called twice-exceptional students).

The last myth I want to specifically mention is the commonly held belief among educators that a student identified as having exceptional needs (e.g., learning disabilities) cannot be gifted. This myth negates the very real cases of gifted and learning-disabled students and allows schools to continue to ignore the needs of giftedness when providing for the disability (Webb et al., 2005). I will focus more on the specific social and emotional struggles of dually exceptional children in Chapter 5.

CHAPTER 2
TALENTS VS. TROUBLES

Gifted children are unique in both their intellectual development and the development of their personality. These attributes, including a strong understanding of the abstract, creative problem solving abilities, and intense emotional development provide a framework of understanding for both parents and educators as they work to identify and assist gifted children (Webb et al., 2007).

Although most of the characteristics that define giftedness are positive, too much of anything can lead to problems. This is particularly true with gifted children, as they wrestle to keep the different parts of their unique personality in balance. We will explore the various aspects of giftedness in the sections below, and relate it back to our three case studies—examining just how problematic some of the normal characteristics of giftedness can be.

THE INTELLECTUAL CHARACTERISTICS OF GIFTEDNESS

The majority of traits that separate gifted children from their peers involve the way in which they intellectually perceive the world. Gifted children often demonstrate exceptional reasoning abilities, leading to rapid learning rates, quick mastery of rote information and a strong capacity to understand abstract information. Often characterized as people who "see" the world in pictures, gifted children typically can intuit solutions to highly complex problems and are very quick to make connections between seemingly unrelated things.

Gifted children also are creative problem solvers, seeking inventive ways to learn and master new information. Prone to a highly vivid imagination, many gifted children are creative in both their use of language and their understanding of the world around them (Silverman, 1989).

In short, these children love to learn, are quick to master the mundane, and actively seek out new and interesting ways to interpret their world.

THE PERSONALITY TRAITS OF GIFTEDNESS

Although giftedness is first defined by the child's intellectual development, there are additional unique characteristics in the areas of personality development. Driven by the intensity of their cognitive abilities, gifted children often have a strong and unyielding need to understand their world. Their strong logical reasoning needs to be reflected in their world in order for them to feel comfortable. As a result, they often have a strong sense of detail and order.

Early moral concern is another typical personality trait of gifted children. This often results in early development of empathy and a mature understanding of the social aspects of the world, including an early awareness of the complex problems facing humanity.

Gifted children typically have a broad range of interests and are intrinsically motivated to learn. However, they also are resistant to taking risks, a trait related to their need to be perfect. Furthermore, they can become easily bored and somewhat rigid in their thinking. If they believe that school or a specific subject is of little value to them, they will become very resistant to the class and may decide it is not necessary to learn the subject at all. This is typical with gifted children and part of the specific personality traits of this population (Webb et al., 2007).

THE EMOTIONAL CHARACTERISTICS OF GIFTEDNESS

Just as gifted children are unique in matters of intellectual and personality development, they are unique with regard to emotional development. These children naturally possess strong emotions that can fluctuate easily between very happy and very sad. They often are passionate in their approach to life, highly empathetic, and overly critical, especially of themselves. Gifted children typically hold themselves, and others, to an impossibly high standard (Silverman, 1989).

Their emotional development also can be characterized as highly intense, something I will be exploring more in Chapter 3. That intensity colors and defines many of the ways gifted children interact with their world—both at home and at school.

Now let's examine how these general attributes of giftedness are demonstrated in school, in their peer relationships, and in the management of their emotions.

CHARACTERISTICS AND SCHOOL

Many gifted children find school enjoyable. Their natural cognitive abilities make learning as necessary as breathing. School offers a source of stimulation and development—an arena in which to explore this aspect of their giftedness.

For some, however, school is not so fun. These gifted children find the routine of school difficult to endure. Pushed toward complex thought processes by the nature of their cognitive development, gifted children are easily bored. This can be particularly true as classrooms focus more and more on the rote information needed for statewide testing and the like. As the curriculum becomes less focused on creative problem solving, gifted children tend to lose interest. Ultimately, this can result in not only disengagement from the learning process, but underachievement and even academic failure.

School also can be challenging related to personality attributes of giftedness. Gifted children often demonstrate a need to be perfect with regard to academic performance. This can lead to some difficulties with risk-taking in school. Sometimes, gifted children will not take classes that challenge them for fear of making a mistake. They may prefer to not turn in an assignment rather than risk making a mistake on that task. This is particularly true if the children perceive the instructions for the assignment as being too open-ended or unclear.

The unique nature of emotional development also can inhibit educational performance, as many gifted children become so worried about their performance in school that they develop physical symptoms: headaches, stomachaches, and similar ailments. These can easily result in a form of school phobia or similar mental health concern that can significantly impact the child. In its most extreme case, it can result in a complete inability of the student to attend school at all.

All of these school-based difficulties are related to the very nature of what it means to be gifted in terms of cognitive, personality, and emotional development.

Let's take a look again at Andrew and see if we can pinpoint the characteristics of giftedness that have led to some of his problems in school.

ANDREW

As you'll remember, Andrew is a sixth-grade student who currently is underperforming in school. When we analyze his case study, we see many of the typical characteristics of giftedness. His incessant need to learn, demonstrated by taking apart electronic toys and an aptitude for computer programming, is typical in gifted children. Furthermore, his immediate boredom with routine activities and eventual disinterest in school also are common within the gifted population.

Andrew began to have significant difficulty as he approached middle school. He stopped turning in schoolwork and struggled with homework completion. His parents attempted all of the school-based suggestions—only to have things get worse. This, too, is a common experience with the parents of gifted children. The strategies schools suggest—a token economy and the like—do not take into consideration the nature of giftedness. For example, a token economy only works if the child is motivated by the token. Most gifted children are only motivated by an innate need to "know." A token economy will not work. Nor will it help the parent understand the nature of the problem, which, in this case, is an apparent mismatch between ability and achievement that has occurred over a very long period of time.

In Andrew's scenario, his academic difficulties are directly related to his need to be mentally challenged, his frustration with rote activities, and his inability to be motivated by external rewards—all of which are very common for these children and relate directly to what it means to be gifted.

In Parts II and III we will examine and practice specific strategies to help Andrew be more successful in school.

CHARACTERISTICS AND PEER RELATIONSHIPS

The nature of giftedness is at the root of some of the more typical problems gifted children face with regard to developing healthy peer relationships. Their need to understand complex concepts, coupled with their keen understanding of the world around them, often can put them at odds with their peers. Although the gifted child wants to discuss the negative impact of global warming, her peers may be discussing fashion trends or the latest musical group. Gifted children may find themselves unable to connect with same-aged children—leaving them sad and confused. Given the nature of their emotional development and the intense way in which they feel things, gifted children may react very strongly to these peer difficulties.

Sometimes the problems do not regard their ability to connect with peers, but are in understanding the subtle social mores of peer interactions, especially in childhood. It is the nature of giftedness to be somewhat rigid with regard to what is "right" and "wrong." The result? Many arguments with peers and adults over subjects about which the gifted child feels he has more knowledge. This is taboo in the social world, as such behavior often is viewed as "bossy" or has other negative connotations.

These particular social difficulties can result in problems making and maintaining friendships. In its most extreme form, these difficulties can result in relational aggression and other forms of bullying. In the worst case, the bullying can then create a cycle that leaves the child unable to function in many aspects of his life and the parent at a loss as to how to help.

In this next scenario we will revisit Meredith and see if her difficulties on the playground were ultimately related to the nature of giftedness.

MEREDITH

Meredith struggles in social situations at school. She often engages in conversations with her peers in which she tells them how to do everything—from the "correct" rules of a tetherball match, to the best way to start a game. Meredith doesn't see that her behavior violates many social mores, nor does she understand why her friends would get upset with her when she is, after all, correct in what she is saying.

What Meredith and her parents fail to realize is that Meredith is simply acting in a way consistent with the attributes of giftedness. She is rigid in her thinking, convinced she is right on just about everything, and insistent that her peers understand their mistakes—all of which are common within the attributes of giftedness.

Her parents are frustrated, not understanding that simply explaining to Meredith why she is having problems will not typically resolve the situation. Meredith must learn to see the world from a different lens—the lens of her peers—if she is going to be able to make a change in her behavior.

Fortunately, there are strategies and ways of communicating to Meredith that can facilitate a positive change in the way in which she interacts with her peers. We will discuss these in the next sections of the book.

CHARACTERISTICS AND EMOTIONS

As discussed in the previous chapter, gifted children are intense—both in terms of their cognitive abilities and their emotional development. Their passion extends to all aspects of their lives. When this attribute is taken to an extreme, they can become tied to their emotional responses to the world, resulting in significant behavioral outbursts. These tantrums can be external, in which the child acts out in some manner: throwing things, slamming doors, yelling, or exercising excessively. They also can be internal, including depression, anxiety, social phobias, or withdrawal from their environment.

More often than not, the intensity of the gifted child's emotional makeup, coupled with his keen ability to see the "big picture" becomes the platform upon which existential distress can form (Webb, 2008). Gifted children begin to deal with difficult world problems at a very early age without the emotional maturity to process such concerns appropriately, leaving them with feelings of frustration and powerlessness. Helping these children learn to manage these intense, global feelings is key to balancing the effect of the existential stressors they may experience. I will delve into this more deeply in the next chapter. For now, let's look at Emily and draw the correlations between her behaviors and the attributes of giftedness.

EMILY

Emily's case history indicates a pattern of high achievement at school. She is a diligent worker, often spending excessive hours in her academic pursuits. She applies that same level of diligence in all aspects of her life. To Emily, success is only measured in one way—achievement.

This thinking is not unusual for high-achieving gifted students. Many times, these children see their talents as requiring due diligence; they *must* achieve, lest their peers discover that they are not as competent as they seem. Furthermore, students at this level do not typically understand how to balance the many aspects of their lives, giving too much of themselves in every situation.

For Emily, the result of this level of performance is painful. She becomes explosive in the home setting from time to time, vacillating from depression to rage within a matter of moments. Emily feels bad about the way she deals with the stressors in her life, but she has no way of changing it: She is not willing to pull back on her achievements, nor does she currently possess the emotional skill needed to navigate through her intensity. This results in a never-ending cycle of stress, frustration, and explosive outbursts.

Emily's pattern of responding to the stressors in her life is very common among gifted students. The emotional passion that helps to propel their achievement also generates the explosive behaviors. In short, Emily is acting in a way completely consistent with her emotional intensity.

The problem for Emily does not lie in the level of her stress or the passion she feels for life. The problems lies in the manner in which she deals with things—the lack of coping strategies and the misperception that she must be perfect in everything in order to be truly smart. Emily equates being smart with being highly successful. She does not yet understand that the two have little in common.

In upcoming chapters, we will look at strategies to assist Emily in the development of the skills needed to reduce her explosive episodes and bring balance back to her world.

Overall, the attributes of giftedness create a unique dichotomy for our gifted children. The aspects of their cognitive and emotional profile, as well as their personality traits, work both for them and against them simultaneously. As a result, gifted children often demonstrate weak social skills and poor coping strategies to deal with the ups and downs inherent in their overall profile.

This dichotomy and the inherent frustration it produces becomes the foundation for many of their experiences at school and at home, affecting the ways in which these children interact with the world. Both parents and educators often are left as frustrated as the children in trying to find the best ways to reduce the negative impact of these difficulties.

NOTES TO THE TEACHER

The characteristics of giftedness have particular relevance to the way in which gifted children function in academic settings. Driven by their intellectual curiosity, these children love to learn—even if they don't demonstrate that in the typically accepted ways within a classroom setting. They are quick to master tasks in school and actively seek ways to interpret the more abstract aspects of their world. Given the routine nature of most traditional "learn and practice" models, it is no wonder that gifted children will sometimes become more of a distraction to the class, as opposed to an active participant, as they try to find meaning in that setting.

Their personality attributes increase the school difficulties, causing perfectionism and a refusal to take academic risks. When teachers assign tasks that appear too open-ended or flexible to the gifted child, she may shut down completely, frustrated that she cannot figure out precisely what the teacher is asking for in the assignment.

The emotional characteristics often leave gifted children unavailable for learning in the classroom, as they wrestle with their ever-fluctuating internal emotional states. Their cognitive passion appears as highly sensitive, overly critical attributes within the context of their emotional development.

This can become even more problematic as the intensity of their emotions combines with their ability to wrestle with larger than life problems. As the class studies global warming, for example, the gifted child may find himself in emotional distress as he fully understands the impact of global warming and his powerlessness to positively impact the outcome.

It is vital that educators have a full understanding of the nature of giftedness when working with these particular students. This understanding provides the framework necessary to enact a teaching philosophy that enables the child to not only acquire the knowledge needed to be successful in the class, but the skills needed to generalize that knowledge and mature into a more fulfilled human being.

CHAPTER 3
TWO SIDES OF THE SAME COIN

Intensity, or overexcitability, as defined by Kazimierz Dabrowski, is an inborn sensitivity or awareness of life. Typically affecting one of five major areas, psychomotor, sensual, intellectual, imaginational, and emotional development, gifted individuals truly view the world through a highly unique lens (Lind, 2001)

Although intensity in and of itself is not a bad thing, it can be frustrating. Most of the problems associated with giftedness are linked to these intensities, especially in the area of emotional development. Like the issues already examined, the origins of this spring from the actual emotional characteristics of being gifted.

Gifted children are intense in all aspects of their lives. They demonstrate a deep level of cognitive reasoning that often is characterized by an almost passionate need to learn. But, this is not the only way in which gifted children are intense. They also are emotionally intense. It is the other side of the same coin—everything that has made this child intellectually intense also has created emotional intensity.

Society applauds cognitive intensity, using words like "genius" and "smart" to describe the passion these kids feel about learning. However, emotional intensity is seldom looked on in the same regard. Children with intense emotions are social pariahs, called "drama queens," "EMO," and emotionally unstable. Gifted children are given the message that while the intellectual aspects of their personality are great, the emotional characteristics—the other side of the coin—make them different, "crazy," or odd.

EMOTIONAL INTENSITY DEFINED

Emotional intensity can typically be described as strong and intense emotional reactions to various situations. Explosive outbursts, crying jags, paralyzing anxiety, or fear are all features of the negative aspects of emotional intensity (Sword, 2006a). But not all emotional reactions are negative or sad. Sometimes the extreme emotions include giddiness, highly frenetic energy, laughter, and general happiness.

Most often, emotional intensity features the frequent vacillation between happiness and anxiety. That's right, mood swings. Gifted children are prone to intense and somewhat erratic mood swings; it is the very nature of their giftedness.

Emotional intensity is not only a matter of mood swings. The intensity also can be demonstrated in physical ways. Symptoms including heart palpitations, blushing, and sensory sensitivity to the environment (e.g., the constant annoyance with the feel of socks or tags in shirts) are all related to emotional intensity. Headaches and nausea, especially in response in school or peer concerns, timed tests, and pressures to perform, also find their root cause in the emotional aspects of being gifted (Sword, 2006b).

Another aspect of emotional intensity lies in a strong affective memory. This refers to a memory of not just the events of a situation, but the feelings associated with the event as well. Gifted children often will relive the feelings of significant moments in their lives, such as a move or the loss of a pet, over and over again. Strong attachments to people and things coupled with their strong affective memory often can make transitions very difficult.

Some of the negative aspects of emotional intensity, aside from the mood swings, include excessive fear in seemingly normal situations, highly critical self-talk, extreme guilt and shame related to perceived imperfections, and the feeling of being out of control. These attributes can have a devastating impact on the everyday functioning of gifted children (Sword, 2006b).

In addition to the emotional aspects of intensity already described, the overexcitablility of their imagination and sensory input can put them at odds with their environment, resulting in significant emotional reactions. Things as simple as the bells indicating the end of lunch period at school or the scratchy feel of tags in clothing can be enough to send the gifted child into an emotional tailspin (Lind, 2001).

EMOTIONAL INTENSITY AND SCHOOL

The impact of intense emotional reactions is not limited to home. Things like the expectation to sit quietly in class, to only speak when spoken to, or to stay on topic when participating in classroom discussions can be exceptionally difficult for the gifted child who is experiencing vacillating sensitivity and excitability toward his environment. Furthermore, the sensory overload of visual stimulation typical of most classrooms can be enough to create a significant emotional response from gifted children.

Emotional intensity also can color the way the child interacts at school related to his own perceptions of success in the school setting. If the child is a high achiever, school is a fun place, despite some of the difficulties his own overexcitability may bring.

If, on the other hand, the child underachieves, school turns into a reminder of the imperfections he possesses—confirmation of his incorrect belief that his failures in school mean he is not gifted at all. That belief, combined with his overall intensity, can lead to significant feelings of self-doubt. In one of its more extreme forms, emotional intensity can lead to a level of anxiety that inhibits a child's ability to attend school. The physical symptoms listed above, coupled with the student's natural intensity, can lead to missing school. Furthermore, generalized anxiety of school performance can lead to full-blown school phobia in a gifted child—all related to emotional intensity.

ANDREW

We've already examined how the cognitive and personality characteristics of giftedness have led to some of the problems Andrew experiences in school. But what about emotional intensity? How does his emotional development contribute to his problems?

Andrew's current struggles in school are likely occurring for the first time in his life. When gifted students struggle they often are forced to confront the perfectionism issues and feelings of guilt and shame they feel. In Andrew's mind he can't be smart if he is struggling. He defines gifted as the high-achieving students he sees around him. It never occurs to him that being gifted and being a high achiever is not the same thing.

Due to the emotional aspects of his giftedness, Andrew makes this problem worse by giving in to the negative self-talk in his mind. He hides or throws away his homework instead of risking getting things wrong—something that would confirm his fear of not *really* being gifted. His natural emotional intensity spins these feelings out of control as he settles into an incorrect perception about his world at school. As a result, he shuts down at home and at school, refusing to connect with anyone regarding academic performance.

His parents continue to try to enforce rules about homework, only to have their best efforts end in a yelling match with their son. Homework becomes a battleground no one wants to face.

Andrew and his parents don't realize the impact of Andrew's emotional development on his current behavior. He is fighting with feelings of guilt and disillusionment regarding his ability to be successful in school. He does not understand that he can use the intensity of his emotions to drive himself into better outcomes at school by learning coping strategies to help when he feels overwhelmed.

EMOTIONAL INTENSITY AND PEERS

Most of the difficulties gifted children face in their peer relationships are related to their intense emotional reactions to everything. Often vacillating between anger and joy, friends find themselves frustrated and unable to predict the gifted child's moods. As a result, friends pull away, leaving the gifted child to try and figure out why.

Problems with peers also can result from the type of relationships most gifted children develop with their friends. Like their emotional and cognitive reactions, their relationships often are very intense. Such intensity, especially in middle childhood, can be overbearing and difficult to manage for both the gifted child and her peers.

Developing friendships with like-minded peers helps to some extent. However, the natural competitiveness of gifted children can be another barrier, intensified by the emotional aspects of friendships. Many times, gifted children experience extremely close friendships that are strained by the day-in, day-out intensity natural to this group of children.

MEREDITH

Most of the difficulties Meredith faces with her peers are related to her extreme behaviors. Her tone of voice and overall demeanor indicate a level of intensity that makes most of her classmates shy away from her. The feelings of loneliness and shame created by these events create a never-ending struggle for her, as she spins on the emotions. The result? A cycle of poor peer relationships that feels unchangeable to her.

Meredith's emotional intensity also has resulted in her peers labeling her as a "drama queen." No one wants to be her friend because they feel that she has to get her way or she will yell at everyone. They come to this feeling naturally, as she has done precisely that on several occasions.

However, her classmates have misunderstood her intent. Rather than acting that way because of a need to be right, she is acting that way as a result of being unable to make herself act differently. She doesn't want to overreact to things or get overexcited when playing. But, despite her efforts to stop herself, she continues to act very emotionally.

Her difficulties changing her behavior has led to her believe that her classmates are correct—she is a drama queen. This feeling creates even more frustration and sadness, causing her to become emotional yet again. Meredith needs to learn that her reactions—not her emotional development—are at the root of the problems with her peers. She needs to learn to mediate her own feelings and control the outbursts.

EMOTIONAL INTENSITY AND SELF-CONCEPT

Most gifted children instinctively understand that they react in unusual ways to their environment. They also are very aware that while they are praised for the cognitive prowess, their emotional intensity is not something appreciated or validated by their peers. Some children grow to believe that they are crazy, or at the very least, overly dramatic.

These children try to force themselves to not react when they are angry, discouraged, happy, or sad. This seldom works, as they simply put off the inevitable explosion. And with each explosion, they receive confirmation that they are not mentally stable—something they want to hide about themselves to everyone. So they then retreat to their rooms and hide the emotional aspect of who they are, afraid that people will find out just how hard it is to be them.

What these children fail to realize is that they are normal. Not normal by the general population's standards, but normal for a gifted person. They can use their natural cognitive abilities to retrain their minds regarding their emotional reactions to the world. They just need to learn how.

EMILY

Emily's emotional outbursts are not just a consequence of her unrealistic expectations or the performance anxiety she feels. They are a byproduct of the intensity of her emotions. She doesn't just get frustrated with the world, she gets *frustrated*. Nothing is done at 50% with her. She is either completely happy or completely sad. Everything functions at 100% or more.

Because she tries to pretend she is not so emotional, Emily saves her frustration for home. At school, she wears a mask of contentment. She allows the world to view her as the perfect student, the perfect friend, the perfect swimmer, and so on.

At home, in the solitude of her room, her mask cracks. Her brain replays every frustration, every mistake, and every negative thought. She spins off the emotions she is finally allowed to feel until they become too much and she explodes.

What Emily, and others like her, don't realize is that her emotions are not something to be ashamed of. It is the intensity of her emotions—her passion—that enables her to succeed as well as she does. She needs to learn coping strategies to handle the stress she puts on herself. Additionally, she needs to learn how to manage the expectations she places on herself.

DABROWSKI'S OVEREXCITABILITIES

As stated earlier, Dabrowski determined five key areas of sensitivity—intellectual, psychomotor, sensual, imaginational, and emotional. We discussed intellectual intensity in the previous chapter. Psychomotor is defined as the demonstration of excess energy. This can include excessive talking, strong physical expressions of emotions, and an intense drive to excel. Sleeplessness also can be an indicator of psychomotor sensitivity. Sensual intensity is centered around the five senses. Tactile sensitivity and a strong need for comfort when upset are common attributes. Characteristics of imaginational and emotional intensity include having strong and irrational fears, daydreaming, vivid and intense dreams, heightened anxiety, and being highly prone to existential depression (Lind, 2001).

Looking at how these specific characteristics impact you and your child can help you figure out the best ways to mediate the more negative aspects of living with such intensity. It is important to remember that being intense is not a bad thing. When developed into its best potential, it becomes the passion people need to find fulfillment in their lives. All too often gifted children are given the message that the intensity of their emotions is something to hide. It is time to give these children the message that intense emotions are not bad. They are simply one aspect of their personalities. Gifted youths need help recognizing that the reaction—not the emotion—often is the cause of the problem. They *can* be taught to react differently.

NOTES TO THE TEACHER

Recognizing emotional intensity in gifted children is as important for the teacher as it is for the parent. By realizing the ways in which your gifted students interact with the world, you as the teacher can better guide and help your students when they run into learning barriers in your classroom. For example, recognizing that a particular gifted student in your class demonstrates intensities with regards to psychomotor (excessive talking), sensual (tactile sensitivity), and emotional (excessive anxieties) domains, you can find ways to help redirect the student without making the child feel worse about her own difficulties.

Without this framework of understanding, teachers are more likely to either deal with the intensity in a punitive manner or negate the child's feeling all together. These types of reactions do more harm than good, as they only serve to reinforce the negative messages gifted children already give themselves about their intensities.

CHAPTER 4
A MATTER OF CHARACTER

A child's personality contributes to the way in which she deals with the world. This is particularly true with gifted children. Considerations including extroversion and introversion, as well as gender, make a difference as to how the gifted child engages with others. These attributes of personality can influence the overall picture of the gifted child and help parents and educators decide the best way in which to help her overcome some of the difficulties she may face.

PERSONALITY TRAITS AND GIFTEDNESS

One of the most misunderstood aspects of personality has to do with the way in which a person interacts with others. This interaction can be broken into two broad terms: extroverts and introverts. Typically, extroverts are thought of as highly social, whereas introverts are thought of as shy people who withdraw from social contact. I actually like to define it differently. For me, these terms have little to do with the behavior we define as shyness. In fact, anyone can be shy in any number of situations. It is not a behavior relegated only to introverts.

I define extroverts and introverts in terms of how the person *renews* at the end of the day. Put another way, does the child seek social contact in order to rejuvenate himself, or does he require solitude? The answer to this could serve as a key toward understanding a child's behavior, as well as the strategies needed to assist in the development of healthy and stable emotional reactions.

EXTROVERSION

Extroverts and introverts experience the positive and difficult aspects of giftedness in different ways. I've already stated that extroverts tend to seek out social contact as a way to renew. For these children, school can be an invigorating place. Classrooms become microcosms of the world at large, offering a comfortable setting for those interested in social interaction.

However, given the nature of bright children, even gifted extroverts can have difficulties in the school arena. Often highly verbal, extroverted gifted children may find significant difficulties in peer interactions as they reach out to their friends, not realizing the social requirements of turn taking in conversations or allowing others to think of games to play. The child who needs the social contact, but is rejected because of behaviors consistent with her giftedness can be left to feel very alone, looking to her teachers and parents for guidance and support.

MEREDITH

Meredith is a great example of a gifted extrovert. As we have already discovered, Meredith's biggest challenge is during highly social activities at school, such as recess and break. She craves social attention, related to her extrovertedness, and is not shy about stating her opinion on things. However, because she lacks many of the skills to function well with her peers, Meredith is awkward in her interactions. She tends to overwhelm her friends with her strong verbal skills and rigid thinking. As a result, she often is shunned. Meredith is left feeling alone, something very contradictory to her need for social contact.

The same difficulty spills into her home life, as she wants to tell her parents every minor detail of her day in an effort to connect and renew at the end of the day. Her mother, however, is more introverted, requiring solitude to renew. Again, Meredith's efforts get thwarted as she doesn't understand why her mom refuses to engage in conversations immediately after school. Meredith is left to feel unheard—something her gifted mind will connect to her self-concept very easily.

The problem is that neither her mom nor Meredith has recognized this aspect of their personalities. Furthermore, Meredith lacks the tools needed to appropriately read the social situation and see when she is either overwhelming her friends or draining her parents. All Meredith sees is that she is trying to connect with people only to have her efforts go unnoticed or worse, ignored.

We will examine some solutions for this in upcoming sections.

INTROVERSION

Introverts often have a bigger problem in the social arena. Gifted introverts have a unique set of needs related to their introversion. They require solitude to rejuvenate, something in scarce supply in most schools. As a result, they retreat from the learning environment, escaping into a book or being alone. Parents are then told that these children have poor social skills or are in *need* of more friends. In an effort to help the child, parents force more social contact, not realizing that it will have the opposite effect, driving the child into greater levels of frustration. Increased frustration in a gifted kid almost always means an explosion in one way or another.

The truth is, gifted introverts learn differently, often needing to observe the world in order to gain meaning from it. Where the extrovert delves into the world for meaning, the gifted introvert often will appear as an outsider (Sword, 2006c). They are, however, as much as an active participant as their extroverted counterparts—they just approach it differently.

ANDREW

Introverted behavior can look like many things in different children. For Andrew, his need for solitude is expressed in his obsession with video games and the computer. He struggles when asked to join group activities at school, finding himself frustrated at the thought of working with others.

At the end of the day, he often needs to be by himself. This worries his parents, who are afraid the solitude is an expression of depression or poor self-esteem. In an effort to connect with him more, his mother always tries to talk about his day the minute he gets home, not realizing that Andrew can't talk at that moment.

From Andrew's perspective, his parents are riding him too hard with their constant questions. He is overwhelmed at the end of the day and needs both quiet and solitude to renew, things in short supply when his mom wants to hear all about his day. He resigns himself to one-word answers to her questions, hoping she'll get the hint and just stop talking.

Andrew's introverted nature creates some problems in both the school and home settings. For Emily, it is a little different.

EMILY

Emily has little difficulty socially. She has connected with a great group of friends who are as smart as she is. More importantly, they understand the pressures she puts on herself and her need for solitude. Their acceptance of her has made school very enjoyable.

However, the introverted behavior has created some difficulties connected with her parents and managing her stress. As an introvert, Emily requires periods of solitude as much as she requires air to breath. Her schedule, however, doesn't allow for necessary periods of respite, as she moves from school, to swim practice, to her job, to . . . the list is endless. All of the activities require a certain amount of social interaction.

After a week or two of her hectic schedule, Emily loses her ability to comfortably interact with her parents and friends. They read this as Emily's "mood swings" and Emily sees herself as a little unbalanced. The reality is something different. Emily doesn't understand her need for solitude—doesn't value it as a necessity in her life. Therefore, she is unable to schedule renewal time into her day. As a result, she pushes herself past her limits and has an emotional reaction—usually a very explosive one.

Emily's story is not unusual. But it is easy to fix. We will explore strategies in upcoming chapters.

No one decides whether or not she is an extrovert or an introvert. And, in fact, one does not have an advantage over the other. The important thing is to understand which one is true for you and your child and appreciate how it impacts your child's demonstration of giftedness.

NOTES TO THE TEACHER

Extroversion and introversion have importance to the classroom setting. As already discussed, classrooms generally are geared for social contact, something very difficult for introverts. It is important for teachers to be aware of how their gifted children interact in class. By understanding whether the gifted child is introverted or extroverted, the teacher can make more informed decisions with regard to grouping, giving opportunities for the child to work alone and assisting in the social development of the child.

Understanding the differences between gifted extroverts and gifted introverts with reference to how they learn also can make a positive difference in how you, as the teacher, choose to work with your students. Remembering that extroverts require direct experiences with their environment, while introverts tend to learn through observation can help you design lessons that will be engaging to all students (Sword, 2006c).

GENDER AND GIFTEDNESS

Boys and girls develop differing opinions about their giftedness as they grow. Males typically see achievement as something external—achieved through hard work. Females, on the other hand see it as intrinsically related to "who" they are. Hard work has little to do with it.

Gender also influences a child's comfort with his or her giftedness. During the elementary school years, giftedness is regarded positively for both boys and girls. However, as children age, being bright takes on different meanings. Peer pressure gets factored in, as well as gender identity. Suddenly being gifted isn't always a good thing.

Society has come a long way with gender equity. However, gifted girls still tend to struggle with their giftedness more than gifted boys, especially during the teen years (Reis & Hébert, 2008). Stereotypes of what it means to be smart—geeks and nerds—often shape a child's willingness to show his giftedness at school or to his friends. The child is again left feeling conflict between who he is and his need to fit in.

BOYS

In many respects, growing up gifted and male is a little easier than growing up gifted and female. Intelligence is respected in boys and seen as a positive attribute. Furthermore, boys tend to associate good grades with strong willpower, discipline, and other positive male attributes. This is particularly true if the gifted boy also is athletic and considered attractive.

But what about the boy who is not athletic? Take the stereotypical math geek—what is it like for him? Growing up gifted can be tough on this guy. With little physical prowess and poor social skills, many of these gifted gentlemen are made to feel bad about their intellectual accomplishments. As a result they often hide who they are, earning poor grades and acting inappropriately as a way to fit in with the peer group to which they want to belong.

Another potential problem lies in the way males attribute success. Typically seen as something outside of their intellect, something born of hard work, boys are more likely to see academic failure and success as a by-product of study habits. They do not associate it in any way with being intelligent. This can work for and against the child, depending on the particular situation.

Let's take a look at Andrew with reference to gender roles and his giftedness.

ANDREW

As we have already seen in previous case examples, Andrew struggles in terms of his grades and work habits. He views this as being related to poor study habits. Although this is true, Andrew also discounts his giftedness, believing that gifted children *never* have difficulties with grades or academic achievement. His state of denial makes it difficult for his family to help coach him at times.

Andrew also has struggled to find a stable peer group in the past. His giftedness and math prowess made most of his classmates see him as nothing more than a math or computer geek. He didn't like the negative connotations of that peer group, so Andrew set out to prove he wasn't like "those kids." He developed skills with video gaming and starting hanging out with kids who weren't doing well in school. In an effort to gain social status with them, he stopped turning in his work. Not being able to get by on innate knowledge anymore, Andrew's grades dropped significantly. This was a problem for his parents, but not for Andrew, as he gained social acceptance as more and more kids stopped viewing him as a geek or nerd.

GIRLS

Gifted girls tend to have a more difficult time as they grow. Like boys, things often are fine in elementary school. Both girls and boys are applauded by peers and adults when they excel in academic endeavors. Even girls gifted in math and science are regarded in a positive light. When interviewed, both girls and boys will indicate liking academic endeavors to an equal degree.

This changes as girls approach adolescence. The opinion of boys becomes more important and peer pressure increases. Girls typically will be less likely to admit they like achieving academically and often will hide their intellect, favoring more stereotypical girl things like music, dance, and fashion. Those who do not acquiesce to the whims of a particular group seen as popular often will be outcast, as the dynamics of girl relationships can be cruel.

Difficulties faced by gifted girls also can relate to how women view achievement. Unlike their male counterparts, girls often see intelligence as intrinsic—something you either have or don't have (Pipher, 1994). As a result, academic failure is personalized. It becomes an indicator of *who* the girl is, not *what* she did. When gifted girls have to study or work hard to achieve something, they view it as proof that they are not gifted at all. They feel like a fraud inside. Given the emotional aspects of their personality, this can have devastating consequences.

EMILY

Emily is a great example of how gifted girls relate academic success to intellectual prowess. In her case study, it is clear that she has found a group of peers that understand and accept her. Gender is not impacting this area, and she is not someone who needs to hide her intellectual abilities from the world.

In fact, the opposite is true. She is driven to excel in all areas of her life, so much so that she cannot handle any form of failure. When she has to study hard for an exam in her advanced course, she sees that as an indicator that she is not as smart as everyone has told her. Furthermore, when she fails at something—whether her extracurricular activities like sports or in academics—she attributes the failure to a problem with how she thinks. It does not occur to her that it is related to other factors. To her, success and failure paint the picture of *who* she is, not *what* she did related to her performance. Everything is personalized, threatening her resiliency, her self-efficacy, and her self-esteem.

For Emily, this personalization of performance contributes to the difficulties she has in managing her behavior, as it leads her to faulty conclusions about her own self-worth. The faulty conclusions, in turn, make it hard for her parents to help her. It is the epitome of a never-ending cycle.

Fortunately, it does not have to be a permanent cycle, as we will see in the later sections of the book.

NOTES TO THE TEACHER

Gender equity in the classroom is not a new topic for teachers. Much research has been put into ensuring that males and females are treated equally in the classroom and have equal representation in classroom materials like textbooks.

What is not typically discussed is gender differences as they relate to giftedness. As stated earlier, boys and girls tend to differ in their attitudes about giftedness as they age, generally showing a decline in their overall opinions about being gifted (Swiatek & Lupkowski-Shoplik, 2000). This particularly is true for groups who already have social integration difficulties—the classic geek stereotype, for example, or gifted girls in high school. Both boys and girls struggle with this in different ways in the classroom. Gifted boys who are not athletic or popular may tend to struggle more than gifted boys who also participate successfully in sports. Gifted girls who are not accepted into specific "popular" groups may struggle with their giftedness more than their counterparts who have found a way to align themselves socially.

Teachers can help smooth these difficulties by understanding the inherent social difficulties with being gifted. Creating a nurturing environment where all students, including those who are gifted, can flourish without looking out of sync socially is the key for many of our bright students. Applauding effort for all students, regardless of gender, and making a conscious effort to portray achievement in a good light also can help.

Finally, it is important to become highly sensitive to the hidden messages the classroom and school settings may be giving our gifted youth. Is giftedness something that is only appreciated if the child is successful? Are there outlets for gifted students who struggle with traditional learning—ways for that child to fit in and find school enjoyable? These questions can help a school find better ways to connect all gifted children to learning. In doing so, both the child and school benefit.

Overall, personality traits do influence the way in which a child demonstrates the characteristics of giftedness. By understanding the impact of personality and gender, parents and educators can better understand the nature of the emotional intensity exhibited by the child.

CHAPTER 5
TWICE BLESSED

Human beings seldom fit into a neat little box—or in this case, label. Gifted children are no exception. As mentioned in Chapter 1, one of the myths commonly held about gifted children is that a person cannot be both gifted and learning disabled. However, giftedness does not preclude being learning disabled, behaviorally disabled, or mentally ill.

Being dually exceptional, or twice-exceptional as it often is called, has its own unique challenges. Not only does the parent need to understand the disability or mental illness of the child, but he needs to understand the unique characteristics attributed to giftedness. All too often children are diagnosed by schools and mental health professionals without any consideration for social and emotional aspects of their giftedness. This often results in a complete failure to fully understand the exceptionalities in light of the basic framework of the child—the giftedness.

GIFTED AND LEARNING DISABLED

School systems typically are good at diagnosing learning difficulties. Systems are in place to seek out and identify students with exceptional needs. School psychologists and psychoeducational assessment teams are fully trained to identify learning disabilities.

This process, however, tends to go askew with gifted children. If the child's learning disability is detected prior to the giftedness, the child is put into the box labeled "learning disability." The fact that he is brilliant may or may not ever be considered in his overall educational programming—something that typically results in more harm than good, as the child begins to believe that he is not at all smart.

If, on the other hand, the giftedness is identified first, an opposite problem occurs. Academic struggles are seen as laziness or defiance, rather than an indicator of a possible learning disability. The gifted child is seldom included in the standard procedure of identifying children with exceptional needs. But the child knows there is a problem. And because the school is identifying it as something within the child's control, he or she may begin to view his giftedness as a lie—something that often can result in a whole new set of problems.

MEREDITH

As we have already determined with Meredith, she is smart and has difficulties with her peers. What we haven't stated is that she struggles with regard to math development. She still functions within the lower limits of her grade-level classroom, but her skills in math are substantially lower than her reading and writing skills. This causes high levels of frustration, as she uses her difficulties to indicate that she is not as smart as everyone thinks she is (remember what we said about girls attributing success and failure to an internal state of being?).

Because she is within the instructional range of the classroom, the teacher is not addressing Meredith's concerns. However, Meredith's parents are very concerned. They spend an excessive amount of time on math homework related to both the difficulty of the work and the emotional intensity that occurs as a result of the stress from the homework. The parents have contacted the school, but because Meredith still functions within the classroom, earning average grades, there is little the school can do.

Frustrated, the parents enlist the help of tutors who drill the rote skills with Meredith and create boredom and more frustration around math. It becomes a lose-lose scenario for everyone.

Unfortunately, Meredith's case has the potential to worsen as the curriculum becomes more and more abstract in the years to come. It is unknown if a true learning disability is the root of the problems she is having. All that Meredith and her parents currently know is that math is hard for her, despite her giftedness.

GIFTED AND MENTAL HEALTH CONCERNS

Gifted children are prone to the same types of mental health concerns as their nongifted peers. However, most mental health professionals are not trained in understanding the unique cognitive and emotional development of this population. This can result in misdiagnosis of various mental health concerns due to the similarity of symptoms between several common childhood disorders and the characteristics of giftedness. Misdiagnosis then leads to mistreatment, as some children are placed on therapy and medication plans based on a diagnosis that may not be accurate (Webb et al., 2005).

The truth is some children are dually exceptional. Many times the mental health diagnosis is given first and the giftedness is ignored, or the giftedness is identified at the expense of the mental health concern. The result can be problematic, as the needs of the child are lost in the sea of labels and treatment plans.

COMMON DIAGNOSTIC PROBLEMS

Some of the more common misdiagnoses occur with disorders whose symptomatology is similar to the characteristics of giftedness (Webb et al., 2005). Mental health disorders including Attention Deficit/Hyperactivity Disorder (ADHD), obsessive-compulsive disorder (OCD), and bipolar disorder are diagnosed through a series of behavioral observations and rating scales. They look at behaviors including impulsivity, "getting into things" at a young age, limited attention, obsessive behaviors, anxiety, moodiness, and depression. Sound familiar? They should. Many of these behaviors also occur naturally as part of the total picture of giftedness. Differential diagnoses are necessary to rule out emotional and cognitive intensity—the main attributes of giftedness. Without such differentiation, it is difficult to ferret out which behaviors are related to the giftedness, and which behaviors can be considered as indicators of mental health concerns. Treatment plans, including both therapy and possible medication, cannot be developed without appropriate diagnoses.

Let's look at Emily's case more closely. Many of her behaviors could lead to a mental health referral.

EMILY

Emily's behavior frequently vacillates between sadness and manic productivity. Furthermore, her anxiety is demonstrated to a high and frequent degree. The key to understanding the nature of these behaviors is to start looking at the setting in which they occur. Emily seldom, if ever, demonstrates anxiety or mood variances at school or at the pool. When she does, it is situation specific, usually involving a need to perform (such as before an important test or meet).

Yet, the extreme behaviors do exist. Emily's parents do enlist the help of mental health professionals, including the school counselor and psychologist. Their initial impression is a mood disorder. They refer Emily's parents to a clinical psychologist, whose initial impression also is a mood disorder.

But is this accurate? Was her behavior examined within the context of her cognitive and emotional profile?

In the next section we will examine various behavioral strategies and Emily's case. This information can assist in differentiating her behaviors between the things we would expect to see given the intensity of her emotional development and things that could indicate a more serious mental health concern. A full analysis of her reactions to behavioral interventions within the context of her giftedness is needed if an appropriate diagnosis is to be made.

DUAL DIAGNOSES

Just because it is difficult to diagnose mental health disorders with gifted children does not mean that all mental health concerns should be dismissed. It takes a trained professional to determine whether or not the particular constellation of symptoms a child is demonstrating is simply related to the emotional nature of his giftedness or a mental illness. In fact, there are several mental health disorders that do occur concurrently with giftedness. And of course, it is the nature of giftedness that can lead to some of these disorders.

One of the more common mental health issues to occur in gifted children is Oppositional Defiant Disorder (ODD; Webb et al., 2005). The nature of their giftedness—their rigidity and strong negotiating skills—often can lead to out of control behaviors. What separates the normal intensity seen in gifted children from the type of intense oppositional behavior seen in children diagnosed with ODD is the level of remorse after the behavioral outbursts. Adaptability to treatment also can help the therapist ferret out the origin of the behaviors associated with ODD and other mental health concerns.

In addition to ODD, anxiety and depression are common dual diagnoses and misdiagnoses (Webb et al., 2005). As we have stated earlier, it is the nature of emotionally intense children to demonstrate periods of high anxiety and depression. However, this can cross a line, warranting medical and therapeutic interventions. Again, a trained professional—one that also is well-versed in the unique social and emotional needs of gifted children—is needed to help navigate through the various possible diagnoses and treatment options.

ANDREW

Andrew demonstrates many behaviors consistent with both ADHD and ODD. His inability to sustain mental effort in school, poor task initiation and task completion skills, as well as his difficulties following rules are synonymous with both diagnoses. However, they also are consistent with giftedness, especially when the child is underchallenged and unengaged in the learning environment.

This is another case where a highly trained mental health professional, one who is well-versed in giftedness, would be very helpful. Analysis of his behavior in the school setting, as well as a thorough evaluation would be helpful in ferreting out the root cause of some of his difficulties. Like Emily's case, evaluating the environments in which the behavior occurs as well as his reaction to specific strategies also could assist his parents in making good treatment decisions for Andrew. Most importantly, working with a team that understands both the possible mental health disorders, as well as the attributes of giftedness, is essential to proper treatment.

Overall, twice-exceptional children pose unique challenges to the parents, the school, and mental health professionals. Everyone involved in the child's life must work first to understand the unique nature of the child's giftedness and second to understand the nature of the other exceptionality—be it a learning disability or mental health concern. Working with professionals in the school and in the mental health industry who look at the child through the lens of giftedness is the key to the successful treatment and educational planning of the child.

NOTES TO THE TEACHER

Dually exceptional children pose a unique problem to education. Meeting the needs of a learning-disabled child who struggles with reading, but who is otherwise gifted requires creative problem solving in the extreme. Teachers need to be flexible and willing to simultaneously enhance and enrich the child's academic experience while also reme-diating the area(s) of deficit. This can become even more complicated when the dual exceptionality is a mental health concern or a pervasive development disorder like autism. All too often the disability takes precedence and drives the educational programming for the child. This may not, however, be the best practice with gifted children. As with anything related to giftedness, it is important to seek assistance from those well trained in both giftedness and the various disabilities within school populations.

The more educational teams can be flexible and creative with regard to overall programming and the more teams can see the disability within the framework of the giftedness, better the outcome for the child.

PART II

GREAT INFORMATION,
BUT NOW WHAT?

CHAPTER 6
LOCATION, LOCATION, LOCATION

Effective parenting often begins first with an understanding of the unique nature of the child, and second with an understanding of how various environments will impact the behaviors and reactions of the child. The child's home and school will strongly influence the ways in which the various positive and challenging aspects of giftedness manifest in the child's life.

Setting a good foundation—one that will support the unique characteristics of this population—is the best way to start managing the challenging aspects of giftedness.

THE NURTURING HOME

The environment in which children spend most of their time is home. Creating a space that allows the child to develop the positive aspects of giftedness while also mediating the negative aspects is the key to effectively parenting gifted children. Chaos, dysfunctional relationships, and poor communication all work against the development of a nurturing environment.

Many attributes contribute to the formation of a well-run household. These include clear expectations regarding behavior, clear consequences, appropriate boundaries, predictable reactions from parents, and opportunities for involvement within the household itself. Let's take each one of these and break them down a little more clearly.

CLEAR EXPECTATIONS FOR BEHAVIOR

The best place to start when creating a nurturing household is in the family's expectations. It is important that every member of the household knows what to expect with regard to chores and homework, behavior toward siblings and adults, and overall behavioral control. In short, it is important to have rules within the family household.

But how many rules? The question is fair enough. Most parents develop systems that are far too rule heavy, meaning there are just too many rules to follow. Adults and children are set up to struggle in that situation.

Likewise, too few rules can have a similar result, as the children have to figure out things on their own regarding appropriate behavior.

I think the question is one more of quality than quantity. A couple of well-developed rules are sufficient to improve the overall functioning of the household. In my house, we use courtesy, responsibility, and respect as an all-encompassing guiding principle. Within those few words, all of the expectations are in place. Our children understand that we, as the parents, will judge their behavior against the backdrop of those words.

Another important aspect to the setting of expectations involves buy-in from the children. The easiest way to enlist their support in this process, especially if you are going from a home with few to no rules to one that is more structured, is to have the children help make the rules. I guarantee that if they are preschool aged or older, they understand the concept of rules and can help make them.

Finally, the guiding principles, rules, or expectations—whichever you choose to call them—must have meaning and merit. They cannot be arbitrary, or your gifted children will ignore and exploit them.

CONSEQUENCES FOR BEHAVIOR

Just as it is important to have clear expectations, it is equally important to have consequences for behavior—both good and bad. For example, if the expectation is that homework must be completed before the TV is turned on, there needs to be a consequence for both compliance and noncompliance. Often there are natural consequences to behavior. When those are too distant or unavailable, it is important to have consequences in place and be able to discuss them with your children. Using the homework example, failure to complete the work results in the natural consequence of no TV time, where compliance results in viewing opportunities.

What if your child acts as though he doesn't care about consequences, but you know better? Stick with it. For instance, if you are certain TV watching is important to your child, keep at it and eventually, the child's desire to watch TV will win out over his need to prove you wrong about the rules.

The key with consequences is positive versus punitive. Positive consequences mean the child can earn things, or not earn things (like time for the TV or computer), based on compliance to the expectations of the household. This type of discipline puts the child in charge of the consequence in that the child "earns" the consequence—good or bad—simply based on behavior. It removes the emotional hook parents often feel with regard to discipline and helps the child learn the connection between her behavior and the outcomes.

Punitive consequences, on the other hand, resort to taking things away in response to poor behavior. It is reactive and seldom teaches the child any other form of behavior. Furthermore, punitive consequences do not tend to motivate the child to behave better, nor do they enable the child to learn *how* to make better choices—two things we want to achieve with discipline. Most studies indicate better outcomes when we emphasis positive disciplinary practices. Worksheet 1, on page 69, includes some questions to ask yourself as your determine if your disciplinary practices are positive in nature.

APPROPRIATE BOUNDARIES

Another key attribute to a healthy family structure involves the establishment and maintenance of boundaries. This means that the parents stay in the role of parent, not friend. They are there to coach and support their child toward healthy decision making. But if the child falters, they also are there to remind her of the rules and expectations of the household and guide her back to compliance. I will discuss coaching techniques in later chapters of the book, but the establishment of boundaries is a critical first step.

Clear boundaries allow children to remain children within the family structure. This is especially important with gifted children as they tend to naturally take on adult roles very early. The clearer the boundaries between all family members, the safer and more secure everyone feels, especially children.

PREDICTABLE REACTIONS FROM PARENTS

One of the most important attributes of a well-run household involves the reactions of the adults to misbehavior from the children. Households in which parents consistently react in a calm, but firm manner tend to yield very positive results with children. Likewise, when parent reactions are random and emotionally charged, children do not learn to manage or change their behavior as easily.

Raising children is always a challenging job, and remaining calm in the middle of an emotionally charged event is very difficult. However,

WORKSHEET 1: POSITIVE DISCIPLINE

1. What is your current method of discipline?
2. Keeping in mind your current discipline strategy, answer the following questions:
    a. Will this teach my child better decision-making skills?
    b. Does the discipline change the misbehavior?
    c. Does this reduce the need for more discipline?
    d. Are you angry when you discipline your children?
    e. Are you impulsive with regard to discipline?
3. What is your goal with regard to discipline?

given the intense nature of gifted children, nonemotional, stable reactions are vital to de-escalating the child when he is having difficulties managing his own behavior.

The key to stable reactions involves knowing, as a parent, your "hot-button" issues—those issues that can elicit a strong emotional response easily. Once the parent knows what these issues are, the development of a strategy to manage the behavior is vital. I recommend taking a *time-away*—a moment of peace to detach emotionally before engaging in the conflict. And you thought time-outs were only for children!

OPPORTUNITIES FOR INVOLVEMENT IN THE HOUSEHOLD

The remaining key attribute of a well-run household involves connecting the child to the home in the first place. In today's world, when families are not as dependent on the contribution of children as they once were, children have fewer opportunities to feel necessary in the running of the household. Chores, participation in meaningful activities needed for the running of the home, and participating in some of the decisions made is one way to give children opportunities for contribution.

Chores are important for children for a number of reasons. Besides teaching discipline and respect for the things they own, chores provide a vehicle for the parents to teach children the importance of their contributions to the running of the house. Remember when your kids were young and wanted to help you around the house? That was an indicator of their natural instinct to connect to the larger picture—the running of the household. Although their interest changes as they realize that helping means more work, the need remains. Chores can answer that need, while teaching several important skills.

Involvement in some of the decisions made in the home is another way in which children can participate at home. Planning a family vacation, helping establish a budget for the cell phone they want you to buy, or creating a new family business to help earn extra money are all ways that children, especially gifted children, can become integral members of the household. Additionally, important life skills can be developed in these tasks that will be needed as the child transitions from childhood to adulthood.

One of the best strategies for providing opportunities for children to participate in the household can be accomplished through the family meeting. More than just a forum for parents to instruct the children on various expectations, consequences, and the like, a family meeting can be a great chance for the child to speak out and share her thoughts regarding the various rules or activities of the household.

Establishing and running a family meeting is easy and can be accomplished with minimal preparation. The key is to have a basis of respect and trust to work from. These attributes will make family meetings more successful. These meetings, when done properly, allow every member of the household to share concerns and contribute to the conversation. They can provide the forum needed to create and maintain a well-run household that promotes healthy emotional development.

CHECKLIST 1: PLANNING A FAMILY MEETING

✦ Establish a time for the meeting to begin. Make sure all household members can attend.

✦ Build an agenda with your children's input. Things you may want to include are:

   ✧ expectations for the meeting,

   ✧ topics,

   ✧ things to celebrate,

   ✧ things to fix, and

   ✧ outcomes.

✦ Remind all family members that the discussion is open, but the final decisions rest with the parents.

✦ Schedule follow-up meeting(s).

Checklist 1 provides parents with some steps in setting up and running family meetings.

Let's take a look at the three case studies as they relate to the home setting. Through their stories, we can see how minor changes to home structure make a big difference.

ANDREW

Andrew's household started off having many rules and very high expectations for behavior. However, as Andrew broke the various rules, it was difficult for his parents to maintain the consequences. Andrew seldom participated in the running of the household and was only required to do his homework—something that was of no importance to him

Later in the chapter, I'll show you how the family adjusted a few things for Andrew, resulting in a positive change for the entire family.

MEREDITH

Meredith had clear expectations regarding homework and chores. She also had clear consequences. Meredith always knew what would happen when she struggled to follow them.

Boundaries, on the other hand, were not as clear. Meredith's mom enjoyed the friendship she had with her daughter. However, her "friendship" often prevented her from being able to appropriately coach her daughter for fear of upsetting her. Furthermore, her mom was so emotionally invested in the difficulties Meredith was having with her peers; she often would cry alongside her daughter. The events at school became bonding experiences between Meredith and her mom—something that created more problems than it solved.

We will look at how Meredith and her mom clarified their relationship later in the chapter. The improvement from such minor changes may surprise you.

EMILY

Emily's family was the epitome of a well-run household. Everyone knew the expectations and consequences for behavior, a family creed hung in the kitchen for the world to see, boundaries were clear, and each child had meaningful ways to contribute to the household. The only problem was in the reactions of the adults to Emily's outbursts.

Due to the intensity of Emily's emotions, both her mother and her father were easily hooked into the drama Emily created. The result? An explosive household that only created more chaos. The parents learned a few simple strategies and yielded major results.

NOTES TO THE TEACHER

Just as the development of a nurturing household provides the framework necessary for positive change to happen, so does the development of a nurturing classroom environment. Gifted students, in

TIP SHEET 1: HOLDING A CLASSROOM MEETING

✓ Think about timing. Trying to hold a meeting right after lunch is not always a good idea.

✓ Limit the time of the meeting.

✓ Choose topics carefully.

✓ Tell the class the goals and agenda of the meeting.

✓ Allow for participation and creative problem solving.

✓ Don't be afraid to try this in secondary education. It can still work to solve many social skills concerns that find their way into the classroom.

✓ Follow up on things discussed.

particular, benefit from an environment that has clear expectations for behavior, clear consequences that utilize a positive discipline approach, clear boundaries, and stable reactions from the teacher. The establishment of this type of environment is not difficult, but it does take both planning and a willingness to see every student interaction as a teachable moment—even the difficult ones.

Most behavior difficulties that occur in the classroom happen as a result of difficulties within the learning environment. Taking the time to objectively look at your classroom setting will not only enable you to see any problems more readily, but it will give you the foundation to help all of your students.

One strategy that can help in the maintenance of a well-run classroom is classroom meetings. Similar to the family meeting, these meetings can be tailored to the specific needs of your classroom, conducted quickly, and used to facilitate the development of social skills in your classroom. Tip Sheet 1 gives teachers some suggestions to consider when planning classroom meetings.

MAKING CHANGE HAPPEN

Knowing the key attributes is only one piece of the puzzle with regard to the establishment of a healthy home that fosters good emotional development. The next step is aligning your own home to emulate those attributes.

The process begins with something I call a Household Inventory. This is a series of questions designed to pinpoint potential areas of concern in the household. It is important to involve the children in this step, as they often can recognize problems very easily.

Completing the Household Inventory (see Worksheet 2 on p. 75) is the first step to identifying the current state of your family. Once the questionnaire is completed, the parents must look for areas to target for improvement and develop a plan. Again, involving the children in this process can increase buy-in and increase the likelihood for success. A good thing to try is to have each child complete the Household Inventory for Children I've included in Worksheet 3 (see p. 76) and use a family meeting to compare the results. Often children will see things as problematic that the parents do not see, and visa versa.

It is important to only target one area for improvement at a time. Otherwise, a plan becomes too difficult to execute with any kind of positive outcome. If the children also have completed an inventory, it is important to reach agreement as a household team on which things to target, keeping in mind parental goals for the household.

Let's revisit our three cases and see how the parents improved the running of the households.

ANDREW

Andrew's parents completed the Household Inventory and discovered weaknesses in the way they handled consequences, as well as his

WORKSHEET 2: HOUSEHOLD INVENTORY FOR PARENTS

1. Clear Expectations

    a. Does every household member know the expectations of the house?

    b. Are there too many or too few rules?

    c. Do the rules have meaning and merit to the family?

2. Clear Consequences

    a. Does every member of the household know the consequences for behavior?

    b. Are consequences dealt with in a positive or punitive manner?

    c. Are the consequences consistently applied?

3. Appropriate Boundaries

    a. Is everyone clear on his or her role within the family?

    b. Are the adults overly attached to the decisions made by the children?

    c. Are the children overly attached to the decisions made by the adults?

    d. Is the line between parent and child clear?

4. Stable Reactions From Parents

    a. Can the children predict how the parents will respond to a variety of situations?

    b. Are the parents consistent in their response?

    c. What are the "hot-button" issues for each adult in the home?

    d. When do the parents get hooked emotionally?

5. Opportunities for Contribution to the Household

    a. Are the children expected to complete chores?

    b. Does the family have meaningful conversations on a regular basis?

    c. Does every member of the household have an opportunity to contribute to the household in some way?

WORKSHEET 3: HOUSEHOLD INVENTORY FOR CHILDREN

1. Clear Expectations
   a. Do you know what your parents' expectations are?
   b. Are there too many or too few rules?
   c. Do the rules have meaning to you?

2. Clear Consequences
   a. Do you know the consequences for breaking a rule?
   b. Are consequences more positive (you earn things) or negative (you lose things)?
   c. Are the consequences consistently applied?

3. Appropriate Boundaries
   a. Do you know your role in the family? Your responsibilities?
   b. Is your parent more of a friend than a parent?
   c. Do you feel like you have to make the rules sometimes?

4. Stable Reactions From Parents
   a. Do you know how your parents will react in various situations?
   b. Are your parents consistent in their response?
   c. What makes your parents really angry? Happy?
   d. How do they act when they are angry? Happy?

5. Opportunities for Contribution to the Household
   a. Do you have chores?
   b. How often do you and your parents have a meaningful conversation about the day or other important things?
   c. How do you contribute to the household?

contributions to the household. The inventory completed by Andrew also demonstrated problems with regard to feeling connected to the family unit. After discussing the results with the family during a family meeting, they collectively decided to change their consequences from punitive to positive and commit them to writing.

Initially, Andrew responded well to the change. But as time progressed, the consequences ceased to have meaning to him and he was soon violating rules. This time, however, the parents reconvened a family meeting and adjusted the consequence procedure. Furthermore, they enlisted the help of the school, something we will discuss shortly.

In the end, there was improvement in Andrew's compliance to the expectations of the household and his understanding of the consequences. They still have a long way to go, but they have taken steps in the right direction.

MEREDITH

Meredith's family also completed a Household Inventory, resulting in some concerns regarding boundaries. Meredith's mother realized that she was very invested in being Meredith's friend. She further realized that the heartache her daughter was feeling was reminiscent of her own childhood experiences. Meredith's mother was not about to let her daughter go through the difficulties she did as a child. So she spent a great deal of time and effort living vicariously through her child in the hopes that she could both prevent her daughter's heartache and heal her own.

As a result of this realization, Meredith's mother stopped associating her daughter's experiences with her own. She started to disengage from the emotional aspects of her daughter's difficulty. Using some of the coaching strategies discussed in the final section of the book, Meredith's mother went from contributing to the problem through loose boundaries and emotional attachment, to facilitating and coaching successful resolutions to many of the more emotional issues Meredith was facing.

As with Andrew, the problem is far from over. But the power in changes made by her mother has set them in a very good direction, laying the foundation needed to more appropriately deal with the emotional aspects of giftedness and the peer difficulties that often ensue.

EMILY

Emily's family took little time to complete the Household Inventory, as many of the basic parenting skills were in place. Through the process, however, they began to recognize the ways in which Emily was able to hook them emotionally. This realization enabled both parents to detach from their daughter's self-inflicted drama. Once Emily was not longer able to elicit such a strong emotional reaction from the other members of the household, she was able to focus more on her own behavioral control.

Emily also completed an inventory, resulting in her opinion that the family was too easy on her emotional outbursts. This information helped the parents realize the depth of Emily's frustration in controlling her own behavior. Strategies, including helping Emily learn her own warning signs and the development of an emotional vocabulary, as explained in Chapter 7, were utilized with positive results. Emily is still overly dramatic in her responses to stress and frustration. However, her parents and siblings no longer participate in her explosions and things deescalate more quickly.

THE SCHOOL ENVIRONMENT

Children also spend a large amount of time in the school setting. Working with the teachers and support staff in schools can help parents support and strengthen the development of happy and successful gifted children.

Most educational systems recognize the unique needs of gifted children. Organizations such as the National Association for Gifted Children (NAGC) and Supporting the Emotional Needs of the Gifted (SENG) have worked hard to change the way in which educators approach this population, publishing books and conducting conferences designed to build both capacity and awareness to the challenges facing gifted children.

Despite these efforts, more work is needed. Working as partners with the school setting, parents can help teachers bridge the distance sometimes seen between the educational system and our gifted youths, especially those who underachieve.

NOTES TO THE TEACHER

Similar to making change happen in the home setting, teachers can use a modified version of the Household Inventory to analyze the classroom setting. This series of questions (see Worksheet 4 on p. 80) can be completed by the teacher or another staff member. There is value in having a trusted staff member complete the inventory along with the teacher, providing the much needed outside opinion on the classroom environment. Additionally, the inventory can be used by the students whenever the teacher is feeling like the there may be some problems with the environment that are causing emotional upheaval in the classroom.

Once the questions are answered, it is important to go through the questions and pinpoint areas for change. As with the discussion of the Household Inventory, target only one or two areas at a time. Small changes often can yield large results.

COLLABORATING WITH THE SCHOOL

Collaboration is the key to successful partnerships between school and home. Developing a common language and maintaining frequent contact is a large part of the collaboration process. This is particularly true if the child is unsuccessful in school, or if the behavior differs greatly between the two settings.

WORKSHEET 4: CLASSROOM INVENTORY

1. Clear Expectations

    a.   Do the students know your expectations regarding behavior?

    b.   Are there too many or too few rules?

    c.   Do the rules have meaning and merit to the classroom and school?

2. Clear Consequences

    a.   Do the students understand the consequences for behavior?

    b.   Are consequences dealt with in a positive or punitive manner?

    c.   Are the consequences consistently applied?

3. Appropriate Boundaries

    a.   Do the students know their role in the classroom?

    b.   Do the students participate in any of the decisions made in the classroom?

4. Stable Reactions From the Teacher

    a.   Can the students predict your reaction to various situations?

    b.   Are you consistent in your responses?

    c.   Do you know your "hot-button" issues?

    d.   Do you know how you react when you get hooked emotionally?

5. Opportunities for Contribution

    a.   Do the students have opportunities to contribute positively to the class?

    b.   Do you try to connect with the students on a regular basis?

Most educators welcome productive dialogue regarding students. However, there are some important things to keep in mind when you, as a parent, are initiating contact with your child's teacher:

1. Teachers have very little time during the school day to discuss issues with parents. Find out the teacher's preferred method of communication (phone or e-mail) and arrange a time that is convenient for both of you to discuss pertinent issues.

2. Teachers often will see your child differently than you do. This is due to the differences between home and school regarding performance requirements, expectations, and peer interactions. Look at a teacher's input as another piece of a complicated puzzle, and factor it into your overall plan for addressing your child's needs.

3. If your child behaves differently at home than school, let the teacher know. Sometimes this can help the teacher understand ways to motivate and coach your child with regard to academic progress.

4. Ask the teacher for advice regarding your child. His unique training and perspective can become a very valuable resource for you.

Tip Sheet 2, on page 82, offers additional guidelines for overcoming communication barriers between parents and teachers.

NOTES TO THE TEACHER

More often than not, teachers are in the position to initiate contact with parents based on concerns they may have about the child. A few points to keep in mind when making that initial contact or when meeting with parents:

TIP SHEET 2: OVERCOMING COMMUNICATION DIFFICULTIES BETWEEN TEACHERS AND PARENTS

✓ Remember that both parties have a vested interest in the child.

✓ Set goals and expectations for the meeting.

✓ Mutual high regard is key. You don't have to agree with each other, but you both must respect each other.

✓ Actively listen to each other.

✓ Keep the child in mind.

1. Parents are always emotionally attached to their children. Getting a call from the school typically has negative connotations and is not always welcomed by the parent. Starting the conversation with something positive can help ease all parties into the conversation.

2. Parents will view the child differently than teachers. This is not because they are oblivious to any of the problems. More often than not, the child *does* behave differently in the two settings. If you can view the conversation as an opportunity to gain additional insight, and not as an opportunity to assign blame, the conversation will be more productive.

3. It is important to be honest with the parent about the child's behavior, while still demonstrating that you care for the child. All parents want their child's teacher to take a positive role in their child's education. Demonstrating to the parent that you genuinely care for the well-being of the student is vital to the development of a problem-solving partnership.

4. Ask the parent for advice regarding the behaviors you see in the classroom. She knows the child better than you ever can, so use her expertise as part of the solution.

5. Remember, you and the parent are on the same side. Both parties want the child to be successful in class. You may disagree on how to achieve the goal, but you will typically have the same goal—and that is a good place to start.

Together, parents and teachers can develop successful home-school communication and environmental supports that can bridge the achievement and behavior gap for some of your gifted youngsters. Collaboration and a mutual regard is all that is required to achieve meaningful results.

ANDREW

Andrew's parents worked closely with the school throughout Andrew's early education. However, in middle school a wedge developed between home and school. Andrew's parents no longer felt supported in their efforts to assist Andrew. They believed the teachers looked at them as lenient parents who did not discipline their child's noncompliance.

Drawing on some of the successful coaching techniques in the area of communication covered in Chapter 10, the parents learned how to communicate more effectively with Andrew's teachers. This resulted in tighter communication between home and school and ultimately more support for Andrew's needs.

Checklist 2 (see p. 84) presents an overview of the steps to build and maintain nurturing environments for the gifted child.

CHECKLIST 2: SETTING THE FOUNDATION

Attributes of a Well-Run Home

✦ Clear expectations of behavior should have meaning for all household members.

✦ Consequences for behavior that focus on a positive, not punitive approach.

✦ Appropriate boundaries where each household member understands his or her role within the family structure.

✦ Stable reactions from the adults in the home.

✦ Meaningful opportunities to contribute to the overall running of the household.

Making Change Happen

✦ Complete the Household Inventory.

✦ Determine areas in need of improvement in overall household structure.

✦ Develop an action plan with contributions from all family members.

✦ Take meaningful action.

The School Environment

✦ Partnership between home and school.

✦ Collaboration with teachers for the good of the child:

    ✧ presumes a mutual high regard for all parties and

    ✧ requires adequate communication between all parties.

CHAPTER 7
WORKING WITH THE
EXPLOSION

One of the most difficult aspects of giftedness is the intensity of emotional reactions by the child, especially to the parents. These children can vacillate from happy to very angry or frustrated quickly, often throwing the entire household out of balance. Typical authoritative parenting strategies often can act as fuel to the fire, increasing the explosive behavior of the child.

Explosions are not always aggressive outbursts of behavior. Sometimes they are more passive, subtle expressions of protest. They can even include anxious and sad behavior. *Explosion*, in this regard, refers to anything that disrupts the household and distorts the emotional functioning of the child.

Gifted children become explosive for the same reasons as their typical peers. They want power and control in their lives, and often will seek it in inappropriate ways until they learn how to attain those things without the extreme behavior. However, gifted children also act out as a result of their emotional intensity. These children can become easily overwhelmed by their environment, reacting in ways that are difficult for parents to manage. Stress from their need to perform at a top level, the frustration of feeling out of control or inadequate, and a general lack of tools in their emotional toolbox to manage these stressors all contribute to their negative feelings until they finally explode.

Fortunately, the same things that led to the behavior—intense cognitive and emotional skills, good reasoning abilities and strong re-siliency—also can be used to help children learn to manage their own behavior.

AVOIDING THE EXPLOSION

The best way to manage the explosive nature of gifted children is to deal with the crisis before there is one. In the last chapter we talked about the importance of setting up the household structure to foster healthy habits in term of communication, family interactions, and disci-pline. Most behavior problems can be abated in that process. However, there are additional things parents can do to prevent a crisis.

DEVELOP A COMMON EMOTIONAL LANGUAGE

Gifted children often lack a way to discuss their feelings. They know they are intense, and realize that they react to the world in ways that are unusual compared to their typical peers. However, they are unable to explain the differences most of the time. Parents can greatly assist this by developing a common language to talk about feelings, especially at a young age. Tip Sheet 3, on page 87, provides advice for parents in helping their children develop their emotional language.

Parents and children need a way to discuss and point out when a child is beginning to lose control. In my household, we use the word *spinning*. Through conversations with each other, my children and I have agreed on a definition for spinning that means *being stuck in a negative emotion and not being able to get out of it*. My children are able to use that word when they need to tell me that they are struggling to

---

TIP SHEET 3: DEVELOPING AN EMOTIONAL LANGUAGE

✓ Work within the developmental age of the child.

✓ Choose words that can cue the child about his or her emotional state.

✓ Choose the words together.

✓ Make sure everyone agrees on the words' meanings.

✓ Be consistent.

---

manage their emotional status. I also am able to use the word when I need to tell them that they are not managing their emotions adequately.

The word itself isn't important. What matters is a common vocabulary with agreed-upon definitions to facilitate a conversation between the child and parent. Developing this has helped my family avoid many explosive moments.

UNDERSTAND THE WARNING SIGNS

Another important preemptive strategy involves teaching the child how to recognize when he is "on the edge"—when he is about to explode. Outbursts rarely happen without warning. There usually are signs to indicate that the explosion is eminent. Using the volcano analogy, we know that feeling earthquakes and seeing ash and trees dying from toxic fumes are indicators that a volcano may erupt. People are the same way, giving many warning signs of the impending crisis. Some of the signs are obvious—an agitated tone of voice, a change in body language, or tears welling in the eyes. Many of the signs are not. One of my former students would yawn and scratch his palms prior to explosive episodes. Another would withdraw from everyone emotionally. A few signs are things felt only by the child, like tension in her neck or sweaty palms. Even a ringing in the ears could signal an increase in emotions.

As with the actual words used in developing an emotional vocabulary, the actual sign is not important. It is the realization that there are signs and that they need to be acknowledged that the parent must strive for. Understanding a person's escalation pattern is an important key to preventing the explosion in the first place.

Most children are unaware of their own escalation cycle. In fact, if you ask the child what she does when she gets stressed, she typically would answer with "I don't know." Helping children figure out how they physically respond to stress is relatively easy for parents to do. I call it the Movie Technique:

1. Start by asking them to pay attention to their physical reactions during a great, high-impact movie. Most children will be able to identify at least two ways in which they respond to adrenaline-rushing, heart-pounding scenes from a movie.

2. Next, ask the child to spend a few minutes the next time she is angry, sad, or taking a test and see if she has any of the same kinds of symptoms. Again, many children will see that their pattern of responding is similar, regardless of the trigger.

3. Find ways for the child to calm her emotions and relax. Parents will need to try several techniques to find the one the works best for the child.

One way parents can implement the Movie Technique is by having kids work through Worksheet 5, provided on page 89. This worksheet helps kids to pinpoint the feelings described above so that they can connect them to their explosive outbursts.

As the third suggestion above points out, parents should try to find different relaxation techniques for children to employ to help them calm

WORKSHEET 5: THE MOVIE TECHNIQUE

1. Watch a high-impact movie or video game and answer the following questions:

    a. How does your body feel during the action scenes? Where do you "feel" the action in your body? Does your jaw tense? Do your palms sweat?

    b. How does your mind feel during action scenes? Are you overly focused? Do you feel tired?

2. The next time you have a test or another stressful activity, think about the following:

    a. Do you have any similar symptoms in your body?

    b. What do you find yourself thinking before a test?

3. The next time you feel strong emotions—happy or sad— ask yourself the following:

    a. Do you feel similar to how you felt during the movie?

    b. What is your mind thinking?

their emotions. Tip Sheet 4 (see p. 90) shows some of the different methods that can be used to promote relaxation and a sense of calm and can be posted in a child's room or locker to help him remember ways to relax, while Worksheet 6, also on page 90, can be given to kids to help them understand how their body and mind should feel when they are relaxed.

Once the child can identify his own escalation cycle, utilization of his emotional vocabulary can help prompt him when he may need to use it.

Other strategies designed to focus on the sensitivity aspects of emotional intensity include understanding the specific ways in which the child interacts with his environment—the specific kinds of over-excitability the child demonstrates. Strategies can then be tailored to the specific needs of the child. For example, if the child has extremes in the psychomotor domain that include excessive talking, developing

TIP SHEET 4: LEARNING TO RELAX

✓ **Deep Breathing:** Take several slow, deep breaths. Imagine the stressful physical symptoms to "melt away."

✓ **Breathing Colors:** Take several deep breaths. On the inhalation, picture your favorite color. I use blue or pink. On the exhalation, imagine a dirty color. This is the color of the stress in your body. Continue slow steady breathing until the color you inhale matches the color you exhale.

✓ **Mini Vacations:** Picture your favorite place in the world. Imagine everything about that place—how things look, how they feel, how they smell. The more vivid, the better.

✓ **Mental Rehearsal:** This is particularly helpful before a test or performance-based activity. Imagine taking each step of the activity successfully. For example, if you are preparing for a piano recital, you may picture getting ready for the recital, walking on stage, sitting on the piano bench, hearing the music in your mind, playing the music perfectly, and hearing the applause at the end. During each step, take several slow breaths to remain calm.

WORKSHEET 6: ARE YOU RELAXED?

1. How does your body feel? Do you have any tension anywhere?

2. How does your mind feel? Are you focused? Tired?

3. How are your emotions? Do you feel calm?

4. Have you tried any strategies to relax? Did they work?

a word used to cue the child when he is talking too much can be highly effective in teaching the child to monitor that aspect of his personality.

What is most important is that gifted children be given ways to understand and work with the unique nature of emotional intensity. The sooner they develop an understanding of their own behavior, an acceptance of the intensity as a natural part of their personae, and the tools needed to monitor and adjust their reactions to things, the sooner they are able to live happily with their intensity.

Preventing explosions, although initially time-consuming, is much easier than trying to deal with the explosion itself. Take a look at the impact of proactive strategies with our case studies.

ANDREW

Andrew's explosions are typically passive—a simple refusal to complete work, not turning in assignments, and the occasional yelling match when he is confronted at home. By utilizing some of the proactive strategies described in this chapter, Andrew's parents were able to reduce the number of times Andrew engaged in the avoidant behavior.

They started with developing a vocabulary. Through the family meetings established in the preceding chapter, Andrew's parents decided to use the word *stuck* to indicate when Andrew was unable to move forward. He also asked to use the phrase *not right now* when he needed to indicate the need for more time before completing the requested task, typically homework.

The use of the words themselves helped, as the family began to talk with each other instead of getting trapped. But it was the discovery of Andrew's escalation phase that proved the most helpful. Using a modified version of the Movie Technique, Andrew discovered that he really hated the nauseous feeling he got when he didn't understand something. In fact, he would do almost anything to avoid it. He also discovered that he feels nauseous often at school and when he worked on his schoolwork.

Working with his parents, he decided to try mental rehearsal and deep breathing as ways to relax his stomach muscles and face the task he was avoiding. His parents also spent time teaching him how to ask for help. They enlisted the assistance of his teachers, and within a few months, Andrew had managed to stop the nausea from occurring. He even started turning in more work, discovering that he knew a lot more than he realized. His grades slowly began to improve.

MEREDITH

Meredith explodes in response to her peers. She also has had outbursts at home when her parents ask her about things related to her friendship difficulties. Meredith's parents carefully worked with Meredith to find words to describe how she felt with her peers. Through this process, Meredith was able to tell her parents that she doesn't hear herself talk and doesn't know when she sounds bossy. They decided to pick a word, tone, which could prompt Meredith at home when she was sounding inappropriate. At school, she worked out a hand signal that her best friend could use when she thought Meredith was sounding bossy. These two things provided a great first step.

In addition to being unaware of her tone of voice, Meredith didn't recognize when she was upset with her friends. She typically told her parents that nothing was wrong at school, even when she was crying. Through increased family meetings and quiet time with her mother, Meredith discovered that she felt very misunderstood by her peers. She measured her success with friends by the number of friends she had, not the quality of the friendships. She also discovered that she carried this sadness in her body, causing hand wringing, tense shoulders, and bad dreams. Using the relaxation techniques described, Meredith learned to release the physical signs of her anxiety using a combination of deep breathing and mini vacations. Meredith reduced the number of outbursts, became more conscious of the tone she used with her friends, and released the frustration and internal pain she felt related to her difficulties with friends. She still only maintains a few close friendships, but she is no longer bothered by it. Nor is she having playground problems at school.

EMILY

Emily has classic tantrums, especially under times of significant stress. She yells, slams the doors, throws things around, and causes significant disruption in the house. But, she also has a lot of warning signs several days before the explosive outburst.

Emily and her family developed a common language to discuss the emotional outbursts. Using the terms *spinning* and *I need a breather,* Emily was able to use her new vocabulary to tell her family when she felt like she was going to explode. Her parents learned to give her time alone, placing no demands on her. They also used the same terms to prompt Emily when they saw the impending explosion before she did.

Emily already knew her escalation cycle. She just didn't think she could prevent the outburst from happening. She had tried deep breathing and exercise, but these did not seem to alleviate the problem. Using the Movie Technique, Emily discovered that she was starting to escalate earlier than she realized. She discovered that her skin literally started to crawl when her agitation started. Using the Mini Vacation strategy and the emotional language she developed with her parents, Emily learned to reduce her anxiety much earlier in the process. As a result, Emily significantly reduced her tantrums.

In this process, Emily also discovered that she struggled with performance anxiety on big tests and swimming events. Using mental rehearsal she learned to manage this aspect of her emotions as well.

NOTES TO THE TEACHER

Proactive strategies are not limited to parenting. Similar strategies can be adopted by teachers for use in the classroom. Knowing your own "hot buttons" as a teacher is key to proactively dealing with potential outbursts in the classroom. Likewise, setting up an environment that has clear expectations and boundaries also will go a long way toward preventing emotional upheaval.

With gifted children, outbursts typically are a response to various stressors the child is feeling. Teaching the entire class ways to relax during tests or when the students are faced with learning challenges is a good way to avoid many of the problems that can arise in a classroom. Techniques including Breathing Colors and Mini Vacations can be performed in a matter of moments without calling attention to a particular student, making them ideal for use in a classroom.

DURING THE CRISIS

Despite good proactive strategies and a lot of training, children will still explode. What parents do during the crisis itself is critical. Handled well, the outburst serves as another opportunity for learning. However, when the explosion is dealt with poorly by the parents, the result usually is a larger explosion down the road.

The key to successful management of the explosion lies in the parents' ability to disengage from the crisis. Often, a situation gets worse because of their reactions to the crisis more so than the initial outburst. This happens for good reason—children know how to push every one of their parents' buttons. Once parents learn to disengage from the emotional aspects of the crisis, the situation usually can be de-escalated quickly.

Disengaging from the crisis starts with an understanding of what the parents' triggers are. That's right, parents have to know their escalation cycle too. Using the same process as was used with children, parents can understand their escalation patterns and learn to diffuse their reactions quickly and efficiently.

But what happens when you are caught off guard? That is where the Time Away Technique comes in:

1. Start with a quick inventory of your feelings as the parent—are you angry, sad, or frustrated?

2. Remove yourself to a quiet area for a moment and utilize one of the relaxation techniques to calm down. You need to give yourself a moment to get back into your logical

brain. When we are in a crisis, that part of our brain stops functioning. Only the benefit of time will reengage logic. Fortunately, a few seconds of calm is all that is required.

3.   Once you are calm, remind yourself of the goal—using the situation as a teachable moment. Decide that no matter what the child does or says, you will not engage. You always have that choice.

4.   Re-enter the crisis from a new, calm, and detached state.

This strategy will place the parent in a position to help the situation instead of making it worse.

Once the parent is able to respond without emotion, it is time to make sure everyone is safe. If the child is hurting himself or others, additional supports will be needed to abate the crisis. But for most situations this simply means putting the child somewhere where he cannot destroy the house or himself.

After the parents have established that everyone is out of harm's way, leave the child alone. If the behavior is an outburst, time is needed to de-escalate the situation. Don't engage. Walk away and let the child calm down. This may take a few minutes. With gifted children, it may even take a few hours. After all, stubbornness is a normal part of being gifted.

Some smaller problems are best ignored. Gifted children often will use their strong verbal skills to say very hurtful things—either about themselves or to their parents during the crisis. This is not the time to address any of it. Staying emotionally detached helps keep the parents from getting hooked into the drama typically created by these kids.

ANDREW

Andrew, despite improvements regarding his homework and school, got into it with his parents one night after receiving a low grade on a difficult test. They questioned him about the exam, trying to figure out what happened. Andrew interpreted their questions as accusations and began yelling, accusing them of hounding him and being mean.

In the past, Andrew's parents would have engaged in the argument, threatening to ground him and take things away. This time, however, they practiced a little detachment, refusing to be baited by their son's harsh words. They remained calm, suggested that Andrew go to his room and settle down, and did not react when he slammed the door.

After about 20 minutes, Andrew came back to his parents, apologized and asked to *start over* (another phrase they established together). His parents asked Andrew to finish his homework and the night continued on.

MEREDITH

Meredith came home from a difficult day at school in tears. Her friends had laughed at her on the playground. She reacted by yelling at them. For the first time in a long while, Meredith brought home a detention for her behavior at recess. Her mother asked her what happened and she responded by bursting into tears and wailing inconsolably. Every attempt by her mother to comfort her was greeted with increased agitation.

Previously, Meredith's mom would have felt hurt by her daughter's reaction. That pain would have led to frustration, which would have ended with her mother yelling at her and sending her to her room.

Things were different this time. Utilizing the relaxation technique of Deep Breathing and Time Away, Meredith's mom was able to control her own emotional reactions. After a couple of minutes, she returned to Meredith relaxed enough to allow her daughter to cry without interference. She escorted Meredith to her room and left her alone.

In a few minutes, Meredith asked for her mother's support. Her mother comforted her and the crisis was over.

EMILY

Emily has made huge progress in managing her behavior. But, she is still prone to angry outbursts, especially when she is tired or under a lot of pressure from finals, swim meets, or other events. These explosions usually take the form of negative self-talk and yelling. In the past, Emily's parents had little patience for her behavior. They yelled back and threatened to withhold privileges.

This time was different. Emily was stressed due to her finals. She came home and yelled at her siblings for asking her a question. She then proceeded to quibble with everyone else in the household. Emily's parents reacted by using one of the phrases—*take a breather honey*—to remind Emily of the procedure to use when she felt out of balance. Emily, recognizing the prompt, went to her room. There was no big explosion, as her parents were able to catch the problem before Emily had gone too far.

NOTES TO THE TEACHER

Time Away isn't just for parents and children. Teachers can benefit for a quick mental time away as well, especially when things have spiraled out of control. Gifted children are challenging to work with at times. This can be particularly true if the student is dually exceptional. When things begin to unravel it is easy for a teacher to lose control—both of her own behavior and of the class. If this happens, the chaos created will only add fuel to the fire. It is important for teachers to give themselves permission to take a deep breath, clear their head, and enlist additional help if necessary.

In addition to finding a place of calm during a crisis, it is important for teachers to utilize de-escalation strategies to reduce the chaos caused by behavioral outbursts and regain control of the student and the classroom. Things like speaking in a calm voice, getting down to the student's level, and looking at the student can all work to relax the student enough to enable the him to regain control of his emotions.

Finally, it is important to help the student back to the routine of the class as soon as possible after the explosion. This prevents the student from using the explosion as a way to get out of completing work. That is not to say that the student will be able to resume the *same* activity. But you will want the student to begin working as soon as possible, whether it be the same assignment or an alternative one.

CLEANING UP AFTER THE EXPLOSION

Most of the time parents are so relieved after the crisis that they don't even think of using the situation as a learning tool. However, this is the best time to review and reteach proactive techniques. Of course this implies that those strategies were initially taught. If they have not been discussed, then that is what must happen first.

The time after the crisis should be used to reflect on the incident. Children often are very tired after a crisis. If they need to unwind or sleep, that is fine. Just as long as the issues brought up by the incident are reflected on within a day. If it goes longer than that, it is really too late. The process of debriefing is fairly simple. I call it the Mirror Technique and it's presented in Worksheet 7 (see p. 99).

Utilizing this technique every time there is a major crisis will teach the child how to be self-evaluative in the future. It also will enable to the parent to see what parts of the proactive skills need a refresher. Tip Sheet 5, on page 99, offers valuable advice for parents to consider during the debriefing process.

Once debriefing occurs, it is time to deal with the rules that were broken before or after the explosion. Just because these are teachable moments does not mean there are no consequences for the behavior. The

WORKSHEET 7: THE MIRROR TECHNIQUE

Have the child answer the following questions:

1. What did you think happened?

2. What were you feeling when it happened?

3. When did you feel like you were losing control?

4. Did you try to de-escalate? What strategies did you try? Were they effective?

Then, the parent should answer the following questions:

5. What did you see happen in the situation?

6. What do you think the child should try next time in order to relax?

TIP SHEET 5: GETTING THE MOST OUT OF DEBRIEFING

✓ Lead the child to an understanding of his behavior without telling him what to think.

✓ Let your child speak first.

✓ Be honest about what you observed.

✓ Allow your child to disagree with you.

✓ Discuss all consequences for the behavior.

negative outcome, whether natural (like a bad grade on a test) or contrived (losing a privilege), should have meaning in order to be effective.

Behavior explosions are always opportunities for learning as the gifted child begins to learn how to manage her sometimes extreme reactions to the world.

ANDREW

Two hours after the behavior outburst, after homework was completed and dinner was eaten, Andrew's parents sat with him and discussed the situation. As a family they reflected on the proactive techniques they had taught and discovered the need for additional phrases for Andrew to use when stressed. They developed new words, discussed how everyone felt using the Mirror Technique, and ended the evening on a pleasant note.

MEREDITH

After Meredith's mother consoled her, she dried her eyes and helped her mom make dinner. Her mother, wanting to make sure the crisis was really over, waited until bedtime to debrief the incident. As she tucked Meredith in for the night, she talked about the detention, Meredith's feelings about being laughed at, and other ways she could have handled her problems. They hugged and snuggled, leaving the day on a good note.

EMILY

Emily's parents came into the room after an hour. She was sitting quietly on her bed. Emily initiated the conversation with her parents, indicating the ways in which she messed up. They discussed as a family how to prompt her to relax. Emily discuss the need to be more preemptive in times of increased stress. In the end, Emily's parents

WORKSHEET 8: BEHAVIOR REFLECTION

1. What did I do?

2. What was my mistake?

3. What happened as a result of that mistake?

4. What can I do next time?

5. What do I think will happen then?

served as nothing more than mentors guiding Emily toward a deeper understanding of her problems.

NOTES TO THE TEACHER

Debriefing is an important aspect of postexplosion clean up in the classroom as well. As with most moments at school, struggling with emotional control is another opportunity for the student to gain the social skills needed to not only become more successful in school, but in life. Utilizing a debriefing strategy consistently goes a long way toward teaching your students the self-monitoring strategies they will need as they approach adulthood.

Debriefing should include a discussion of the behavior that occurred and the consequences. The next step is a discussion of the preferred behavior and consequences. Finally, a plan to move the student from the nonpreferred behavior to the preferred behavior should be developed.

Debriefing is not something that needs to take a long time to complete. In fact, a simple worksheet (see Worksheet 8) that is reviewed between the teacher or support staff and the student may be enough to help our gifted children begin to learn to analyze their own behavioral responses and make adjustments.

QUICK REFERENCE GUIDE

Checklist 3 provides an overview of the steps to prevent, manage, and clean up after an explosion.

CHECKLIST 3: WORKING WITH THE EXPLOSION

Preventing the Explosion

✦ Develop a common vocabulary for discussing the child's emotions.

✦ Determine the escalation cycle of the child (and the parent).

   ✧ What are the physical warning signs that the child is feeling stressed?

   ✧ What are the most effective techniques for de-escalation?

✦ Develop a plan with the child to remain in a balanced emotional state.

During the Crisis

✦ Disengage from the emotional aspect of the crisis.

✦ Make sure everyone is safe.

✦ Allow for a "cooling off" period before trying to re-engage the child.

✦ Remember, some things are best ignored.

Cleaning Up After the Explosion

✦ Remember, all explosions are teachable moments.

✦ Debrief and strategize.

✦ Administer consequences, either natural or contrived.

CHAPTER 8
UNIQUE PERSONALITY ISSUES

Basic parenting strategies rooted in an understanding of the unique needs of gifted children are enough to deal with most issues that arise. Character traits such as introversion, as well as the complex problems facing dually exceptional children often can increase the problems faced by teachers, parents, and children.

In this chapter, we will examine a few of the unique situations and review specific strategies to address them.

EXTROVERTS AND INTROVERTS

As we discussed in Chapter 4, extroverts and introverts approach the world in unique ways. This is particularly true when the additional layer of giftedness is added. Extroverts, well suited to the complex social nature of school, often find solace as it appeals to their innate need for social contact. However, a layer of giftedness can complicate matters, as the intensity of their behaviors often creates a barrier between them and their peers. Many times, gifted youths are unable to build the connections they crave.

The problem can be a complex one to fix, as gifted children usually are unaware of their own behaviors. They view the world from a somewhat rigid lens, not understanding how unique their point of reference is. When they are rejected by peers, they interpret it as a rejection of *who* they are, not necessarily *what* they did.

One of the more successful strategies I've used with kids to help them understand the impact their behavior has on others is a modified version of the Movie Technique presented in Chapter 7. The basic premise is the same, but instead of looking for the physical symptoms of stress, the child is paying attention to the characters and their reactions to one another. The parent can be involved by helping the child discover the connection between the behavior of one character and the reaction of the others. The parent can then relate that back to the original situation and dissect the reactions—both from the child to her friends, and from the friends to the child. By going through this process, a gifted child learns how her behavior generates specific reactions from others.

Development of an emotional language is another important key to managing the possible negative aspects of giftedness and extroverted behavior. Utilization of an emotional language to openly discuss the problems, express frustration, and strategize solutions can mean the difference between positive peer experiences and negative ones.

As discussed in Chapter 4, gifted introverts struggle with the social aspects of school to a greater degree. They require more support than their extroverted counterparts in dealing with their behavioral outbursts. Often comprised of public and private personae, gifted introverts typically require built-in periods of solitude. Cooling off periods, opportunities to decompress, and strengthening of a personal understanding of themselves is needed in order to mediate the frustrating world these children live in.

Gifted introverts approach the world from two different perspectives (Sword, 2006c). If they are not shy, they will engage publicly, appearing confident in many social situations. They have learned to compensate for their need for solitude by taking control of their environment. As a result, many gifted introverts do not realize just how introverted they are—something that can lead to explosive behaviors if they have not incorporated opportunities to decompress into their day.

These same children often learn by watching others (Sword, 2006c). This natural observation strategy can be used to help them understand the emotional toll taken when they forget to give themselves permission to relax in solitude from time to time.

Teaching gifted children to relax is key to improving their ability to control the behavioral outbursts that sometimes occur. Strategies including Mini Vacations and Breathing Colors outlined in Chapter 7 are very effective in this situation as well.

Let's take a look at the three cases presented throughout the book and evaluate the effectiveness of some of the strategies in these cases.

ANDREW

As we learned earlier, Andrew in an introvert. His mother, realizing Andrew's need for solitude at the end of the day, stopped demanding that Andrew engage in a conversation about his day immediately after school. Instead, she offered him 20 minutes to cool off by himself.

Furthermore, Andrew's mom discovered that she and her son renew in opposite ways, as she is much more extroverted. This discovery was an "Ah-ha" moment for his mom. No longer obsessed with making sure Andrew was constantly engaging with others, Andrew and his mom were able to come to a compromise regarding Andrew's friendships and engagement with the family.

MEREDITH

As we discovered in Chapter 4, Meredith struggles in her peer interactions, despite her overwhelming need for them. This has created a dichotomy for Meredith—one that she struggles to reconcile.

Using the modified Movie Technique, Meredith's parents guided her through an understanding of the behavior of some of her favorite movie characters. The next time she had trouble with her peers, they walked her through the same process, helping to point out the connection between some of her behaviors and the reaction from the kids.

A lot of work still needs to be done in this area, but Meredith is slowly beginning to discern the impact of her behavior on others. Consistent coaching in this regard should result in a more positive outcome as she learns to monitor and adjust her own behavior.

Meredith and her mother have also discovered why they struggle to communicate with each other. This realization has brought them closer, as they developed a way for Meredith to connect with her mother.

EMILY

Emily's introverted nature comes out in her need to renew. She overextends herself socially, forgetting her need for solitude and quiet. Her parents addressed this with her by reinforcing the relaxation techniques from Chapter 7. Now, Emily schedules time to renew and relax, carving out a few minutes throughout her school day and at home for a Mini Vacation. The result has been almost immediate, as Emily reduces the times she pushes herself beyond her personal limits.

NOTES TO THE TEACHER

Extroversion and introversion have implications for the classroom. As we have stated earlier, these aspects of personality color the way a gifted child interacts with the learning environment. When the extrovert is bored during lectures because she craves a more hands-on, interactive approach, the introvert is learning. But, when group projects and peer-share opportunities are assigned, the extrovert is thrilled while the introvert is struggling just to remain calm. It can be a daunting job meeting the needs of these diverse learners.

Knowing your students is the key to achieving a balance between the various types of learners in your classroom. This is particularly true with gifted learners. It may require letting go of a few of your beliefs about giftedness. Not all gifted kids demonstrate their intellect in overt ways. Many shy away from outward demonstrations of their passion for learning, choosing instead to ease into the learning environment. This can become even more intense when the emotional aspects of giftedness are factored into the equation.

Planning a broad range of lessons that enable both extroverted and introverted learners to grow and develop can enable you to reach more of your students. Flexible groupings also can help ensure that all learners are given opportunities for meaningful experiences in your class. It is a bit more work initiating this type of learning environment, but the long-term impact is more than worth it for both the students and for you.

DUALLY EXCEPTIONAL CHILDREN

Dually exceptional children often experience increased frustration due to the way in which both parts of their personality interface. The learning-disabled, yet gifted child, for example, often will underperform because of frustration related to the inability to express her ideas at school as a result of her learning disability. This frustration can create a continuous cycle of poor task initiation at school, which ultimately leads to more arguments in the home setting. Strategies to address both the learning difficulties and the frustration are required if a positive change is going to be made.

Learning difficulties are best addressed through collaboration in the school setting. By maintaining consistent communication with the school, adjustments to the workload can be handled with little difficulty.

Dealing with the frustration can be more difficult, as the gifted child often associates performance with intelligence. Because they struggle with learning, many gifted children make the assumption that they are not smart at all or that their weakness permeates all aspects of learning.

Teaching the child to discern between accurate mental messages and inaccurate messages is vital if success in this area is going to be gained.

One method that helps the child learn to discern correct from incorrect information is a strategy I call Proof:

1. Start by asking the child to identify what she believes about her learning and school (see Worksheet 9 on p. 109). Make this as specific as possible. Ask clarifying questions as needed.

2. Once the child is able to identify the mental messages she holds about her ability to complete her work, ask her to find proof or evidence that the message is correct. This must be tangible evidence that can have no meaning other than confirming the mental message she is holding about herself.

3. If she finds proof, help her analyze the accuracy of the proof.

4. If she does not find proof, help her create a new mental message about her own competencies.

MEREDITH

We learned in Chapter 5 that Meredith struggles with regard to math. Although her skills are still within the instructional range of the classroom, Meredith interprets her difficulties as proof that she is not smart overall. She allows her frustrations to rule the logical part of her mind, resulting in several incorrect mental messages.

Her parents used the Proof technique, coupled with the relaxation strategies discussed in Chapter 7. This resulted in a clearer understanding of her actual learning challenges. Meredith was able to focus on the truth of her difficulties, without lumping unnecessary problems or ideas into it.

WORKSHEET 9: HOW DO YOU KNOW?

1. Do you think you are good at (FILL IN THE BLANK)? Why or why not? Be very specific.

2. What proof can you find to support or disprove your position? For example, if you think you are lousy at math, what grades do you get on your tests? How about your classwork? What is your performance on your standardized test scores?

3. Now that you KNOW something and are not ASSUMING, what can you do to change the outcome (if you want to)? Be specific.

4. If you discovered that your original ideas were incorrect in some way, how can you change them? What are your new ideas?

NOTES TO THE TEACHER

Meeting the needs of dually exceptional children can be very difficult. Fortunately, there is help available. Members of the IEP team (if applicable), or other support personnel often can provide you with specific strategies for working with these unique children. It is important, however, that the child's giftedness never be forgotten or pushed aside in an effort to accommodate the other exceptionality. Giftedness, as we have already learned, is so much more than simply learning things at a fast rate. It impacts the way in which the child interacts with his world. It is as much a part of his makeup as his physical body. As such, it must be considered when making any decisions. You, as the teacher, may have to partner with the parent to ensure that this happens.

GIFTED AND MENTAL HEALTH CONCERNS

Mental illness is another complex issue facing parents. Gifted children often are misdiagnosed because of a poor understanding of the nature of giftedness. Those who are appropriately diagnosed often are inappropriately treated for similar reasons. Parents are placed in the position of advocate, needing to ensure the proper diagnosis and treatment for their children.

One way to help with the differentiation between behaviors associated with giftedness, and those that may indicate a larger problem is by keeping a journal of both the behaviors and the strategies. Adding the outcome of the strategies to your list can enable a trained mental health professional to get a bigger, better picture of the needs of your child and determine whether or not the behaviors warrant additional interventions.

In the next chapter, we will look at specific ways to find a mental health professional to help with this process.

NOTES TO THE TEACHER

Working with mental health issues in a classroom environment can be very tricky. When the child is also gifted, it can seem like an impossible task. As with other exceptionalities, there often are many support personnel available to assist you with this type of student. And as previously discussed, it is vital that you factor in giftedness when deciding how best to meet the needs of a gifted student with mental health concerns.

Flexibility and a willingness to find creative solutions are the most important factors for teams to keep in mind. These children often will require highly specialized educational plans; being open to many types of solutions is the best way to find a win-win situation that can meet your needs as the teacher, as well as the needs of the student.

QUICK REFERENCE GUIDE

Checklist 4, on page 112, presents a way for parents and teachers to monitor their abilities in understanding and working with unique personalities and character issues.

CHECKLIST 4: UNIQUE PERSONALITY ISSUES

Extroverts and Introverts

◆ Extroverts require social contact to rejuvenate.

    ✧ May have difficulties in peer interactions.

    ✧ Use modified Movie Technique to assist the child in understanding the connection between his behavior and the reaction of his peers.

    ✧ Develop an emotional language to talk about feelings.

◆ Introverts require periods of solitude in order to renew.

    ✧ Cooling off periods are needed immediately after periods of prolonged social contact, like school.

    ✧ Specific relaxation strategies, including Breathing Colors and Mini Vacations, need to be built into the gifted introvert's day to assist in maintenance of emotional balance.

Dually Exceptional Children

◆ Gifted and learning disabled

    ✧ Address learning struggles through direct collaboration with the school.

    ✧ Use the Proof strategy if the child is unable to recognize personal strengths or if the child is receiving inaccurate mental messages.

◆ Gifted and mental health considerations

    ✧ Enlist the help of qualified professionals well versed in the unique needs of gifted children.

    ✧ Maintain a journal listing the behaviors, strategies, and reactions utilized with and by the child. This journal will help the mental health professional with regard to a differential diagnosis.

CHAPTER 9
YES, IT REALLY DOES TAKE A VILLAGE

Parenting is an exhausting job—and parenting gifted children carries a level of frustration that is seldom understood. Parents often are left feeling inadequate to help the problems facing their kids, with little support from others.

Educators, mental health professionals, friends, and family all can serve a role in helping both the parent and child navigate their way through this difficult time. But finding these resources can be challenging, especially if you don't know where to look.

WORKING WITH SCHOOL PERSONNEL

Collaborating with the school can feel intimidating for many parents. Often at a loss for how to proceed, a wall forms between the parent and the teacher. This is especially true if your child has difficulties learning or with behavioral control.

We examined a few tips for collaboration with the school setting in Chapter 6. Using the same basic ideas of mutual high regard, professionalism, and partnership, parents can develop a strong network of support with the school and develop a plan for helping their child improve both at home and at school.

Mutual appreciation is the cornerstone to successful collaboration with the school. Regardless of the particular situation you find yourself in, it is important to appreciate the expertise of most teachers in the field of learning. Equally, it is important that teachers and other educators appreciate the parents' expertise with regard to their own child.

Professionalism goes hand in hand with respect. As stated previously, it is important for parents to respect the limited time teachers may have to discuss issues in class or on the phone. As with any professional, make an appointment to speak with them, scheduling a period of time devoted to problem solving issues concerning your child.

Teachers are the best first contact with the school. However, it is important to recognize that there are other professionals that may prove helpful. At the school level, the coordinator for gifted education (if there is one), counselors, school psychologists, and administrators are all possible resources.

CREATING A PLAN

Most schools have a process to assist struggling students. This same process may be appropriate when the difficulty is behavioral or emotional, instead of academic. The first step in initiating this process is to contact the teachers. Once that has been done, and a conference or meeting is scheduled, the team (including parents, teachers, and support personnel) must create a plan.

Typically this begins with clarifying the strengths and areas of weakness the child presents. It is important for parents to offer suggestions in this process, clarifying their own concerns for the child.

Once concerns have been identified, it is important to establish what the goals are for the child. These goals are an opportunity to not only clarify the direction the team should head in, but also build consistency in terms of expectation and consequences.

After concerns and goals have been addressed, it is important for

TIP SHEET 6: HOW TO CREATE AN EDUCATIONAL PLAN

✓   Consider the goals of all parties.

✓   Discuss the child's strengths first.

✓   Problem solve those areas of difficulty the child is experiencing.

✓   Decide on measureable goals to focus on.

✓   Keep it simple.

the team to discuss interventions that have already been utilized to address the problems, as well as the effectiveness of those interventions. All too often teams look at interventions without ever discussing the known effectiveness of the strategies attempted.

New strategies should be discussed and a plan put into place. It is important to make the plan easy to follow and replicate across multiple settings. In other words, the plan should be able to be implemented in the environments where the difficulties occur. Follow-up timelines should then be established. This is another area where the collaborative efforts between home and school sometimes falter. Information about the effectiveness of the intervention strategies should be collected and given to the team at the follow-up meeting.

Sometimes teams disagree as to how to best meet the needs of the child. In these cases it is important to remember the team's goal to help the child and approach problem solving with an open mind. Tip Sheet 6 shares some considerations that should be at the forefront of a team's mind when creating an educational plan.

Let's see how this process could work using one of our case studies.

ANDREW

As we already know, Andrew has been struggling for a while. His parents have attempted many strategies to help, all with varying degrees of success. The school team has attempted interventions as well, most of which have not worked. At this point, Andrew continues to struggle.

In an effort to "circle the wagons" and help Andrew be more successful, his parents initiated contact with school personnel. After several conversations with his teachers, a meeting was arranged. The parents were initially very concerned about the meeting, afraid that they would be thought of as bad parents. However, using the Proof strategy outlined in Chapter 8, the parents came to the realization that they had no reason to be worried over the meeting.

The team itself consisted of the teachers, Andrew, his parents, and a counselor. The counselor's role was to facilitate the meeting, while the teachers and parents each contributed to the development of the plan. The team identified both successes and areas in need of improvement. They also discussed previous interventions and their effectiveness.

Before new interventions were discussed, the parents asked the teachers to discuss goals for Andrew. The team followed suit, and specific goals were adopted. Andrew was part of the process, contributing to the buy-in that would be needed during the implementation phase.

Finally, a new plan was developed for Andrew, using strategies that built on past successes. A follow-up meeting was scheduled and the plan was implemented.

In terms of effectiveness, many of the strategies, combined with the things the parents were doing at home, proved helpful in teaching Andrew new coping skills at school. But it was the consistent communication and collaboration that facilitated Andrew's success.

Andrew's case is a great example of a team of people coming together with a common goal of helping a child—it is magic when it works well.

A Word on Alternative Education

Not all parents choose traditional education for their children, either in a public or private setting. Many choose homeschooling options. Although many of the difficulties that face gifted children in the traditional learning model can be negated in a homeschooling or alternative educational system, it is still important to know how to access assistance if it is needed. In particular, it is important to have a good understanding of giftedness and a close working relationship with the individuals educating your child.

Parenting groups can be a great resource for parents in any setting. With traditional education, parent groups often can be found through the school district. They are sometimes site specific, and other times function as a larger group for the district as a whole. The purpose of these groups typically is limited to informing parents about the gifted program within the district. Some groups also provide trainings and newsletters to parents, sometimes geared toward the social and emotional aspects of giftedness.

Alternative education programs usually have resources they can connect parents to or strong parent groups. It is important for parents utilizing this model to connect with these groups just in case additional support and assistance is required at a later time. Most of these groups are formed for the purpose of helping parents understand giftedness and the unique social and emotional needs of their children.

Parent groups can be an important source of comfort for support as parents deal with the more extreme aspects of giftedness in their children. The groups typically meet with some regularity and cover the basic aspects of giftedness, parenting, and the specific needs of the group. Homeschooling organizations and school districts often can be a good place to start looking for parenting groups. If there are none in your area, you can start your own group. The Recommended Resources section at the end of the book gives a few reference materials that are

TIP SHEET 7: STARTING A PARENT GROUP

✓ Contact your local school district first to see if there are groups in your area.

✓ Contact other parents of gifted children to start a group.

✓ Decide on a meeting place and time. Establish group norms or rules.

✓ Establish group goals—learning, support, or enrichment.

✓ Utilize resources like those found through http://www.sengifted.org to provide a framework for meetings.

✓ Be creative. Invite guest experts to come and speak to help publicize your group.

good for use with parenting groups. Tip Sheet 7 also provides some suggestions for parents on starting their own parent group.

Parent support need not be limited to face-to-face contact. More and more resources are springing up online in social networking sites like Facebook and Twitter, as well as numerous blogs. Developing a network of support can help prevent parent burnout and enable you to realize that you are not alone in your efforts to cope with your gifted child's intensity.

WORKING WITH MENTAL HEALTH PROFESSIONALS

It can be very difficult for some parents to enlist the help of mental health professionals. However, there are times when this is exactly the sort of help parents may need. The key is finding one with a solid understanding of gifted children and emotional intensity.

I recommend starting with referrals from friends and school person-

TIP SHEET 8: FINDING AND WORKING WITH A MENTAL HEALTH PROFESSIONAL

✓ Get referrals, if possible, from other parents of gifted students.

✓ Interview the professional—ask about his beliefs regarding the impact of giftedness on behavior and mental health.

✓ Ask for periodic updates regarding your child.

✓ Trust your instincts—if something feels off for you and your child, it may not be a good fit between you and the professional.

✓ Remember, things often get worse before they get better. Don't expect a quick fix for your child.

nel (see Tip Sheet 8 for more recommendations regarding finding and working with mental health professionals). Once that list is reconciled with insurance and financial considerations, it is important to interview each mental health professional being considered. This can help ensure both a foundation in gifted children, as well as compatibility regarding therapeutic style.

Examples of appropriate questions could include the following:

1. What is your understanding of giftedness and emotional intensity?

2. How do you prefer to work with children? Are there specific kinds of strategies you find most effective?

3. Do you work with the whole family system, or just the child?

4. How do you make differential diagnoses?

TIP SHEET 9: HOW TO KEEP
A BEHAVIOR JOURNAL

✓ Decide which behavior(s) to target.

✓ Write down each behavioral occurrence, including what
happened immediately before and what happened immediately
after the behavior.

✓ Be sure to indicate if there are any changes in strategies used
with the child, including changes in medication use.

✓ Keep a daily log initially. Work with the mental health professional
to determine when to pull back to weekly tracking.

This list is by no means meant to be exhaustive. It is merely something to initiate the interview process.

Once a partnership is established between the mental health professional and the family, it is important to understand treatment goals and guidelines. It also is important to establish the way in which the professional would like to address the evaluation of treatment effectiveness. As mentioned previously, maintenance of a journal chronicling the effectiveness of various strategies can be extremely helpful to the entire team. Tip Sheet 9 provides advice on keeping a behavior journal.

The therapeutic process itself can be tumultuous at times. It is important for the parent to understand that this is a normal part of the process and is not necessarily an indicator that things are getting worse. In this situation, the parent should discuss his concerns with the mental health professional. Problems and disagreements are best worked out through open communication.

Overall, mental health professionals can provide significant support to the parent and child. Utilizing their services can prove to be beneficial to all concerned. Making a lasting change for the family and the child often requires involvement from many people, but the end result is worth it.

QUICK REFERENCE GUIDE

Checklist 5 shows an overview of the steps parents should use when working with others to help their child.

CHECKLIST 5: THE TEAM APPROACH

Working With School Personnel

+ Start with mutual high regard for all parties involved with your child.

+ Discuss the goals you have for your child and ask the teacher(s) to explain his goals.

+ Develop a plan for working with the child that is consistent across settings.

+ Review the plan periodically for effectiveness.

+ If there is disagreement, work through the concerns with an open mind.

Working With Mental Health Professionals

+ Interview qualified personnel working with your child.

+ Ask about the therapeutic and treatment practices.

+ Don't be afraid to ask questions.

+ If you have a concern, discuss it with the professionals involved. Change will only happen when there is a partnership between all parties.

PART III

BEING YOUR CHILD'S COACH—SPECIFIC STRATEGIES

CHAPTER 10
WHAT MAKES A GOOD COACH?

Coaching your child is a little different than the typical authoritative role that parenting and teaching often implies. Coaching moves away from telling a child what to do, and focuses on giving him or her the tools necessary to independently figure things out (Cook, 1999). By using effective communication and empowerment strategies, a good mentor can help the child understand his own uniqueness and fully develop his potential. Good coaches also lead by example, are flexible in their thinking, view behavioral challenges and problems as a process of growth, and are motivational in their approach.

Parents are in a great position to act as coaches to their child, teaching everything from understanding the unique characteristics of giftedness, to coping strategies, to managing the intensity that comes with being gifted. Likewise teachers are in a natural position to assume a coaching role, helping the child to develop the skills needed to integrate the positive aspects of his intensity into his daily routines at school. Teachers also are in good position to assist in the refinement of the self-monitoring skills gifted children need to learn in order to manage their intensity.

QUALITIES OF AN EFFECTIVE COACH

Effective coaching requires a unique skill set. Fortunately, it is an easy one to learn. Many of these abilities are similar to the strategies outlined for effective parenting. Coaching, as opposed to parenting, simply takes it one step further by focusing on the empowerment and cognitive training of the child. Let's take a look at the specific qualities inherent in successful coaching.

Communication

The first step toward positive coaching is effective communication between the parent (mentor) and the child (mentee). This includes (a) being able to listen carefully to the words spoken by the child, both verbal and nonverbal; (b) appropriately expressing your needs, wants, and concerns to the child; and (c) overcoming the typical roadblocks to appropriate dialogue with your child. When these three things occur regularly in the home, everyone is able to participate in an environment that says "you are valued."

Being able to listen to your child's spoken and unspoken words requires the parent to be quiet. This isn't simply quieting your vocal abilities—it also is quieting your mind. Many times we are wrapped up in the busyness of the day. We don't listen actively to our children. And we miss both the verbal and nonverbal communication they are sharing. We rush from activity to activity, with scarcely a few moments in which we can truly connect with our family. When this happens regularly, we begin to build a barrier between us and our children, blocking effective communication. Unfortunately, this wall remains in place, even when we need to communicate something important to our child.

Breaking down the communication barrier starts with an awareness of active listening and silence. We must make it a priority to spend time quieting our minds after an active day and transition to family time. By doing this we not only reap the benefit of being able to hear about our children's lives, but we model ways to transition in and out of various environments.

●◆ TIP SHEET 10: ACTIVE LISTENING

✓ Remain quiet when your child is speaking—including your mind.

✓ Focus on your child during the conversation.

✓ Listen with your eyes as well as your ears.

✓ Help your child develop an emotional vocabulary to assist with his or her communication (see Chapter 7 for more on this).

Active listening extends beyond the listening we do with our ears. To pick up on the nonverbal cues, we must listen with our eyes—noticing the subtle changes in behavior that occur when our child is happy, excited, or under stress. By heightening our sensitivity to this form of communication we increase our ability to recognize the things our child may be hesitant to speak directly about. Tip Sheet 10 provides some strategies for practicing active listening.

A great example is the child who comes home with a bad report from the teacher. He may avoid eye contact, shuffle through the backpack "pretending" to look for something, or say he left his things at school—all to avoid having you discover the parent note sitting in his notebook. If we are paying attention to the nonverbal signs he is giving us, we can recognize that there is something he does not want to say, and we can take measures to prompt it from him.

Effective communication does not end with active listening and the recognition of nonverbal signals. It also involves being able to clearly and unemotionally communicate your needs, wants, and desires to the child. It's not as easy as it may sound.

Children are experts when it comes to understanding what makes us, the parent, lose control. This particularly is true with gifted children. They are able to assess our emotional states and determine the right time to pick an argument—the time when we are likely to respond poorly.

Our job, when this happens, is to maintain our emotional cool and stay somewhat detached, at least emotionally. When we are able to do this, the emotional power play ends and we are better able to communicate our needs to the child again. The following chapters will demonstrate this more clearly through the use of role-plays and dialogue samples.

Sometimes we hit roadblocks when we try to communicate with our children—either from them or from the self-imposed blocks we construct. These roadblocks prevent us from being able to understand our children or express our needs. As a result, both parties often are left frustrated and emotionally spent. Fortunately, roadblocks can be anticipated and avoided with a little work.

The most common roadblocks built by children include the following:

✦   whining and other forms of crying;

✦   yelling, name-calling, or shaming the parent; and

✦   refusing to speak or diverting attention.

There are others, but the majority fall into these categories. These work because they all tend to throw the parent into an emotional response, either due to guilt (as in the case of crying behaviors), anger (related to yelling and other forms of disrespect), or complete frustration (when the child refuses to engage at all).

Overcoming these roadblocks must start with emotional detachment. It is critical that the parent learns to distance her emotions from the situation so she does not get hooked into a response that only serves to decrease communication. Additionally, prompting the child for the response you are looking for and reminding the child of the consequences of his choices also help to break through the communication barriers established by children.

We will use some of these roadblocks in the dialogue samples in the next few chapters. Through the examples, the subtle changes in communication can be better illustrated.

Just as children build barriers to effective communication, so do parents. Most of the problems can be categorized in the same way:

✦ crying styles of communication that include name-calling or shaming;

✦ angry communication that includes threats and commands; or

✦ withdrawing from the conversation, including making judgments, diverting, and prematurely ending the conversation.

These blocks have the same negative impact as they do for children, preventing either side from being heard. Tip Sheet 11 (see p. 130) provides some suggestions for overcoming communication roadblocks.

Overcoming roadblocks to communication involves both being aware of your own emotional status and the way in which you may be coming across to the child. This is not something that can be achieved from a chaotic place. The parent needs to be calm, centered, and focused for effective communication—and good coaching—to occur.

FACILITATION

Facilitation refers to the act of assisting in the progress a person makes toward a specific goal (Cook, 1999). In the case of parenting, it means helping your child achieve a desired outcome without doing it for him. Homework time is a great example of facilitated learning when we are doing it well. In that scenario, we are on hand to answer questions, provide feedback, and cue the child, but we do not complete the homework ourselves, nor do we provide answers for the child.

Effective facilitation requires a framework of consistency and bal-

TIP SHEET 11: OVERCOMING COMMUNICATION ROADBLOCKS

✓ Overcome the child's roadblocks including whining, yelling, and ignoring forms of communication:

 » Remain calm; keep your emotions out of the equation.

 » Clearly and concisely state the desired outcome.

 » Remind the child of the consequences for good and poor decisions.

✓ Follow through on everything.

✓ Overcome the parental roadblocks including threatening, making judgments, and shaming:

 » Stay focused on the goal of effective communication.

 » Keep emotions out of the equation.

 » Become hyperaware of personal word choice when communicating with your child.

 » Use clear and concise language when possible.

 » Remember the goal!

ance in our home setting, as discussed in Part II. When our household runs well, clear boundaries are developed and maintained, and clear expectations are obvious, we are well positioned to facilitate our child's learning. This particularly is true when we are assisting our child in the acquisition of the tools necessary to monitor and regulate his behavior.

In addition to a well-run household, parents need a strong framework of knowledge regarding the unique aspects of giftedness. This will help when trying to model or cue your child toward more effective emotional responses to various situations.

The act of facilitation itself focuses on teaching the child how to think, not what to think. This is a significant change for many parents,

TIP SHEET 12: FACILITATING LEARNING

✓ Start with the fervent belief that your child can master his emotions.

✓ Have a thorough understanding of the nature of giftedness.

✓ Focus on the process of making a good decision, not the decision itself.

✓ Use modeling and cueing as a way to lead the child to appropriate decisions.

✓ Always debrief after positive and negative emotional periods.

who are used to telling the child what he did wrong, how to improve, and how to prevent future errors. In short, most of us spend a lot of time telling our children what to think.

By contrast, effective coaching, and specifically facilitation, focuses on modeling and cueing the child to come to decisions on his own. Instead of explaining what the child did wrong, facilitation requires that parents ask the child to think through his own thought process, asking probing questions like "What mistake do you think you made?", "Why was it a poor choice?", "What happens when we make that kind of a choice?", and so forth. This process enables the child to learn the exact things that led him to whatever result he achieved. And it can provide the framework to help him make a new set of decisions. A guide to good facilitated learning can be found in Tip Sheet 12.

With gifted children facilitated learning particularly is effective because it makes use of their superior logic skills as an avenue to retrain their emotional responses. Furthermore, it helps the child learn to become more aware of why he makes the decisions he makes and deliberately choose a new response—definitely a win-win for everyone involved.

Facilitation typically is achieved thorough the following types of strategies:

- ✦ **Modeling:** This occurs when the parent or child is shown a specific way of doing something. Role-playing various scenarios is a great way to model a specific type of response.

- ✦ **Prompting or cueing:** Typically this relates to guiding the child toward the answer you are looking for without specifically telling the child. This way, she is forced to go through the cognitive steps on her own.

- ✦ **Reflection or debriefing:** This refers to the postexplosion period, when the parent and child review the decisions that lead to the explosive behavior and develop a plan to prevent future explosions. Specific techniques for this are discussed at length in Chapter 7.

Use of a combination of these strategies will effectively teach a gifted child how to navigate through the maze of her emotions in a manner that leaves her feeling confident and resilient, instead of defeated.

Inspiration

The final major quality required in effective coaching is inspiration. Just as communication and facilitation moved the child away from negative patterns of thinking and toward functional thought processes, the goal of inspiration is to motivate the child to continue a pattern of growth. Inspiring parents believe profoundly in the ability of their child to overcome any difficulties set before them. They are their child's own personal cheer squad.

This doesn't mean parents should be unrealistic. If the child failed to get in a college application on time, no amount of cheering is going to change the fact that she will not be considered for admission.

⊶ TIP SHEET 13: INSPIRING OTHERS

✓ Start with unconditional positive regard for your child.

✓ Fully commit to the growth process, understanding that there will be setbacks.

✓ Never lie to your child, but always believe that the child will persevere through any adversity that he or she may face.

✓ Take time to rejuvenate yourself when things get really difficult.

✓ Build quality one-on-one time with your child into your life.

✓ Remember all of the reasons you love your child.

However, it does mean that the parents believe in their child's ability to overcome the heartache caused by the mistake the child made. It also affirms the parents' belief that their child will learn from the mistake and make a new set of choices in the future.

But inspiration does more. It becomes the rock the child will lean on when she struggles to move forward. Inspirational parents are committed to the growth process of the child and inherently know that the child will be resilient enough to manage whatever happens in her life. This type of inspiration can mean the difference between lifelong resiliency for the child and poor coping strategies. Tip Sheet 13 provides some advice for parents on how to inspire their children and others around them.

NOTES TO THE TEACHER

Teachers utilize many of the more typical aspects of coaching quite naturally in the classroom. Utilizing the same techniques as previously discussed—communication, facilitation, and inspiration—teachers can do more than simply teach curriculum to their students. They can help gifted children move closer toward their own potential while simultaneously minimizing the more difficult aspects of teaching this unique group. Let's take a brief look at each area of effective coaching and apply it to the classroom setting.

COMMUNICATION

As already discussed, communication is the cornerstone to effective coaching. In the classroom setting this is even more important, as gifted children can easily come across as know-it-alls or disrespectful in their communication style both with peers and adults.

It is important for teachers to remember where this behavior originates—that the very characteristics of giftedness, namely the deep-seeded need to know things, contribute to some of the communication styles of gifted children. Effective listening and communication is needed if the teacher is going to discern when the child is acting out versus simply asking for more information.

In order for the teacher to effectively listen and communicate with gifted students, teachers must take the time to quiet their own minds and agendas and focus on the student. This can be very difficult as the teacher typically is focused on the lesson and getting through the large amount of material that has to be covered in a day. But being quiet and mentally "present" is really the only way to hear the actual questions from the student.

Sometimes, our gifted children will ask questions that are inappropriate to the lesson at hand. This usually stems from their own need to know things at a significantly more thorough depth than their peers. When this happens, it is important for the teacher to make time to talk with the student. Tell the student you need to move on, but be sure to follow up with the student and get to the questions. In doing that, the student's needs will be met, and the connection between teacher and student will be enhanced.

Effective communication between teachers and students also can prevent many of the little behavioral outbursts that can happen in a classroom. Taking the time to hear and understand the student is the first key step toward creating an environment that enhances the learning of all students.

Facilitation

Facilitation is the most natural role of a teacher. Education is goal directed, and teachers inherently help students move toward the specific goals and objectives of the various lessons. What's important to remember is to help the student without doing it for him.

This can be a bit tricky as all students often will find ways to gets their needs met by others, without having to do some of the work themselves. Teachers need to be wary of this, looking for those teachable moments when children can be taught how to do for themselves. A great example of this can be the student who is bored in class and asks for additional work. When we constantly furnish that work without thinking, we are missing opportunities to facilitate a greater learning chance for the student. In this scenario, instead of just providing enrichment directly, we can ask the student to design a project that can serve as an enrichment activity. In doing this, we are showing the student how to get his own needs met.

As with parent facilitation, the concept of teachers as facilitators takes some initial groundwork. Consistency, clear and effective rules for behavior, and trust all are essential within the classroom environment in order for a teacher's attempts at facilitated learning to be effective. And as stated before, a strong basis of knowledge regarding the unique characteristics of giftedness also is vital.

Facilitation is really about teaching children how to think. In today's culture, what could be more necessary, especially for our gifted students? Merely providing children with the information required under state and federal guidelines isn't enough. Gifted children need to be given opportunities to generalize that information in new and creative ways—all of which happens quite organically when teachers are good facilitators.

INSPIRATION

Finally, effective coaching requires being an inspiration to your students. Just as effective communication and facilitation techniques serve to help the child become more functional in his learning, inspiration motivates the child to continue learning—even when things get difficult. Inspiring teachers set a learning environment where risk is expected and safe. This is key to the act of learning and one of the more difficult things for gifted children with regard to scholastic endeavors.

Setting a framework of hope and the strong belief that the child can persevere and be resilient in his learning is vital if gifted children are going to move past their inherent perfectionism and take academic risks. It is in these risks that real learning occurs. The teacher that can harness that willingness to take academic risks and inspire her students to follow her, even if it is uncomfortable, has done more than teach a few important facts. She has set the stage for lifelong learning for her students.

QUICK REFERENCE GUIDE

Checklist 6, on page 137, includes an overview of the qualities necessary for effective parent-driven coaching and tips on achieving it.

CHECKLIST 6: WHAT MAKES A GOOD COACH?

Effective Communication

◆ Understand the child's needs and wants.

◆ Clearly express your needs and wants.

◆ Actively listen to the child.

◆ Look at nonverbal and verbal communication.

◆ Deal effectively with roadblocks to communication.

Effective Facilitation

◆ Teach the child to recognize, understand, and redirect emotionally intense feelings and behaviors.

◆ Utilize modeling and prompting strategies to help children learn.

◆ Focus should be on teaching children how to think, not what to think.

Being a Source of Inspiration

◆ Strong commitment to the child and his growth process.

◆ Walk with the child through the difficult times.

◆ Use motivation as a tool to propel the child in the right direction.

◆ Provide the foundation needed to navigate through the hard times.

CHAPTER 11
RELATIONSHIP ISSUES

Relationships are difficult in the best of situations. This particularly can be true with gifted children, as the rigid nature of their thinking patterns and the overly sensitive emotional nature of their personality can cause conflicts with both peers and adults. Typical relationship issues, including developing healthy friendships, bullying problems, trying to "fit in," and handling peer pressure, are appropriate topics for role-playing and parent coaching.

HEALTHY RELATIONSHIPS

Developing healthy friendships can be difficult for gifted children. Many times these children struggle with social skills, resulting in poor interpersonal communication and poor friendships. Take the following scenario. How would you help your child navigate through it?

SCENARIO

Your child received detention at school for yelling at a classmate during recess. You discover the detention when going through the backpack the next morning.

INITIAL PARENT-CHILD DIALOGUE

> *Parent:* Jessie, what is this?
>
> *Child:* Nothing. Just a stupid detention. Becky told the noon-duty I was yelling at her. But she lied.
>
> *Parent:* Well that doesn't seem like Becky. Did you yell?
>
> *Child:* Yes, but it wasn't my fault.
>
> *Parent:* Jessie, you always say that. But if you were yelling, it is your fault.
>
> *Child:* But . . .
>
> *Parent:* I don't want to hear it. You have to stop getting mad at your friends, sweetie. Or you're not going to have any friends to yell at.
>
> *Child:* You never listen to me. (Child bursts into tears and runs from the room)

ANALYSIS OF DIALOGUE

In this scenario, Jessie is having difficulties controlling her anger and expressing herself to her friends. The dialogue between mother and daughter does nothing to help Jessie understand why yelling resulted in a problem and a detention. Let's look at the specific problems with the dialogue.

> *Parent:* Jessie, what is this?
>
> *Child:* Nothing. Just a stupid detention. Becky told the noon-duty I was yelling at her. But she lied.
>
> *Parent:* Well that doesn't seem like Becky. Did you yell?

The parent's word choice conveys the message that her child is not telling the truth. Although this may be true, the way this is stated presents a major roadblock to communication and guarantees a defensive response.

> *Child:* Yes, but it wasn't my fault.
>
> *Parent:* Jessie, you always say that. But if you were yelling, it is your fault.

Again, the word choice prohibits a true dialogue from occurring. Although the child needs to be coached on how to accept responsibility, dictating *what* the child is supposed to think doesn't teach the child how to figure this out.

> *Child:* But . . .
>
> *Parent:* I don't want to hear it. You have to stop getting mad at your friends, sweetie. Or you're not going to have any friends to yell at.

The parent is no longer interested in the excuses of the child. This presents a major roadblock to communication and prevents the child from learning through this experience.

> *Child:* You never listen to me. (Child bursts into tears and runs from the room)

NEW DIALOGUE USING COACHING STRATEGIES

Using successful coaching techniques, as well as some of the strategies previously mentioned, let's see how this scenario can be improved.

> *Parent:* Jessie, what is this?

> *Child:* Nothing. Just a stupid detention. Becky told the noon-duty I was yelling at her. But she lied.
>
> *Parent:* What exactly happened honey?
>
> (This gives the child a chance to tell her part of the story.)
>
> *Child:* Becky wasn't playing nice on tetherball. She kept cheating. I told her to stop and play right or I wasn't going to be her friend anymore. Then she went to the noon-duty and told her I yelled. But mommy, I didn't yell. Honest.
>
> *Parent:* Is it possible that it felt like yelling to her?

This asks the child to look at the impact of her behavior on others. When this becomes a regular part of the dialogue the child learns to evaluate the impact of her own behavior.

> *Child:* I guess. But she didn't have to tell on me. I don't want to be her friend anymore.
>
> *Parent:* I understand how you feel, but let's not decide friendships right now. Let's stay focused on the detention. Sometimes when people are mad, their voice gets really loud. Is it possible that yours got loud—even if you didn't mean to yell?

The parent redirects the child to the actual problem without letting the conversation deteriorate. She provides examples and guides the child to a particular way of looking at her behavior.

> *Child:* Yeah, I guess so.
>
> *Parent:* So, is there a different way you could have handled this without being angry with your friend? One that didn't result in yelling?
>
> (Again, the parent is prompting and guiding the child.)
>
> *Child:* I tried talking to her, but she didn't listen.

●◆ TIP SHEET 14: CONFLICT RESOLUTION SKILLS

Teach your child to do the following:

✓ Calm down.

✓ State the problem using "I" statements.

✓ Allow the other person to state her perspective.

✓ Each person needs to "own" his or her part of the situation.

✓ Brainstorm a solution.

✓ Thank the person for helping to solve the problem.

Parent: So, if she wasn't listening to you, what else can you do to solve the problem?

From this point the parent can continue teaching and guiding the child, coaching, until the child has the problem solved and has determined a new solution to the problem. Tip Sheet 14 has some suggestions for teaching children conflict resolution skills.

BULLYING

Bullying happens in a variety of ways and for a variety of reasons. Gifted children are not immune to it, finding themselves in both the position of the bully and the victim. The extreme emotional nature of gifted children makes dealing with bullying particularly difficult, as the situations often deteriorate rapidly and lead to a host of other problems including significant anxiety and depression.

The following scenario presents the gifted child as the victim of bullying. It is important to note that giftedness can lead to bullying behaviors just as easily.

SCENARIO

Your child tells you she is scared to go to school because her best friend is being mean. This happens on the same day that her best friend's mother has called you and told you that the girls have been fighting at school. The other parent is concerned that your daughter is treating her daughter poorly.

INITIAL PARENT-CHILD DIALOGUE

> *Parent:* Emma, what's going on between you and Shelly?
>
> *Child:* I don't want to talk about.
>
> *Parent:* We have to. Her mom called and said you guys are fighting.
>
> *Child:* It's no big deal. But I don't feel well. Can I stay home?
>
> *Parent:* No, you have to go to school. But why is Shelly's mom calling if there isn't a problem? I need you to tell me what's going on.
>
> *Child:* (Child gets angry and starts to yell) I told you—nothing's wrong. I just can't go to school. Please mom. I can't. (Child starts crying inconsolably)
>
> *Parent:* Look, you can either tell me what's going on or not. But either way, you have to go to school.
>
> *Child:* Fine. But I hate it there. And I hate Shelly. (Child runs out of room and slams door to bedroom)

ANALYSIS OF DIALOGUE

In this scenario, Emma is having problems with her friend and no longer wants to attend school. The other parent is involved, asking Emma's mother to talk with Emma. The dialogue that ensues does not move Emma toward a clear discussion of her feelings or result in a plan to deal with them. Instead, both mother and daughter leave the conversation feeling powerless. Let's look at the specific problems with the dialogue.

> *Parent:* Emma, what's going on between you and Shelly?
>
> *Child:* I don't want to talk about.
>
> *Parent:* We have to. Her mom called and said you guys are fighting.
>
> *Child:* It's no big deal. But I don't feel well. Can I stay home?
>
> *Parent:* No, you have to go to school. But why is Shelly's mom calling if there isn't a problem? I need you to tell me what's going on.

This initial phase of the exchange starts well. The parent asks good questions and sets an appropriate boundary. However, her demand for information could lead to a highly defensive response from Emma.

> *Child:* (Child gets angry and starts to yell) I told you—nothing's wrong. I just can't go to school. Please mom. I can't. (Child starts crying inconsolably)
>
> *Parent:* Look, you can either tell me what's going on or not. But either way, you have to go to school.

Although this may appear fine initially, as the parent is staying detached and setting an appropriate boundary, she is not making use of the opportunity to teach her child about the connection between her feelings and the friendship situation. Without the information such a conversation could deliver, the parent cannot know how to proceed.

> *Child:* Fine. But I hate it there. And I hate Shelly. (Child runs out of room and slams door to bedroom)

The child has ended the dialogue completely in this scenario—with nothing resolved and a bigger emotional concern.

New Dialogue Using
Coaching Strategies

Using successful coaching techniques, as well as some of the strategies presented earlier in the book, let's see how this scenario can be improved.

> *Parent:* Emma, Shelly's mom called and told me you guys are having some problems. What is going on with you guys?
>
> *Child:* I don't want to talk about.
>
> *Parent:* It sounds like she has made you pretty mad. Sometimes talking about it can help.

The parent is cueing her daughter as to her apparent feelings without "naming" them directly. If the child has learned to develop an emotional vocabulary, this may be enough to cue her that she needs to regulate her moods a bit.

> *Child:* It's no big deal. But I don't feel well. Can I stay home?
>
> *Parent:* Staying home isn't going to make your feelings go away sweetheart. Why don't we try to figure out the problem and see if we can talk about it?
>
> (Here the parent is setting a boundary and providing the roadmap needed to solve the problem.)
>
> *Child:* It's too hard mom. (Child starts crying)
>
> *Parent:* (Parent consoles child) I know, baby, but we have to face the problem or it will only get bigger. Did Shelly hurt you yesterday? Did you argue?

●◆ TIP SHEET 15: REPORTING A BULLY

✓ First clarify what a bully is and is not with your child.

✓ Determine if the school has an anonymous way to report bullying. If it does, allow the child to use that format. If it does not:

   » Determine a "safe" time to talk with the administration of the school.

   » Encourage your child to always report incidents of bullying.

✓ If your child is the victim of bullying, be sure to spend time teaching the child how to work past the negative impact of the bully.

✓ See the Recommended Resources pages for more information.

In this setting, the child is more likely to respond positively and begin to speak about the problem. Once the child begins to talk, the parent can guide her to a solution to try and get her to school—without the drama of the previous dialogue.

Emma's case seems to be more of a problem of two friends arguing, but in some cases, gifted children can experience more painful bullying. Tip Sheet 15 provides parents with advice for reporting bullies in their child's school.

CONFORMISM AND PEER PRESSURE

Nothing screams preteen and teen like peer pressure. With gifted children, the push for "normal" can be intense. And the more intelligent a child is, the further away from normal he or she often feels. This creates internal stress that eventually can result in underperformance at school or participation in risky behaviors, simply for the opportunity to fit in.

Scenario

Your child is failing at school. His standardized test scores are high, and he is doing all of his homework. Yet nothing is being turned in and he is failing several of his classes.

Initial Parent-Child Dialogue

> *Parent:* Eric, I got a call from your teachers today. They said you haven't been turning in your work all semester. What's going on?
>
> *Child:* It's no big deal, Mom. I can bring the grades up by the end of the year.
>
> *Parent:* That's not the point. You are failing your classes now. What are you doing with the work, Eric?
>
> *Child:* (Says nothing)
>
> *Parent:* Eric! I am speaking to you. What is going on? (Parent's voice is raised)
>
> *Child:* It doesn't matter Mom. I told you—I'll bring up my grades.
>
> *Parent:* It does matter. And I don't want to hear it. Get the work turned in now, or I'll make sure you just fail the year and repeat it. (Parent storms off)

Analysis of Dialogue

In this scenario, Eric does the homework but doesn't turn it in, resulting in grade problems. The dialogue does not elicit responses that are going to solve this particular problem. In fact, this piece of dialogue results in little to no communication at all. Let's analyze this a bit:

> *Parent:* Eric, I got a call from your teachers today. They said you haven't been turning in your work all semester. What's going on?

> *Child:* It's no big deal, Mom. I can bring the grades up by the end of the year.
>
> *Parent:* That's not the point. You are failing your classes now. What are you doing with the work, Eric?

The parent is no doubt very frustrated with Eric's choices. This frustration easily bleeds into the tone of voice, typically putting the child on the defensive.

> *Child:* (Says nothing)
>
> *Parent:* Eric! I am speaking to you. What is going on? (Parent's voice is raised)

Now the parent is in argument mode. From this point on, the focus is not on problem solving, but being right. This is true for both the child and the parent.

> *Child:* It doesn't matter Mom. I told you—I'll bring up my grades.
>
> *Parent:* It does matter. And I don't want to hear it. Get the work turned in now, or I'll make sure you just fail the year and repeat it. (Parent storms off)

Obviously this is a no-win situation. The child is not going to change his behavior—and neither is the parent. Both are fully entrenched in their need to be right in this situation.

NEW DIALOGUE USING COACHING STRATEGIES

Using successful coaching techniques, as well as some of the strategies previously mentioned, this scenario can have a positive end.

> *Parent:* Eric, I got a call from your teachers today. They said you haven't been turning in your work all semester. What's going on?
>
> *Child:* It's no big deal, Mom. I can bring the grades up by the end of the year.
>
> *Parent:* I am sure that you can, and you already know that Dad and I expect passing grades. I am more concerned with why this is happening. You do your homework every night, right?

The parent has established the boundary and expectations, while refocusing the conversation toward problem solving.

> *Child:* Yes.
>
> *Parent:* OK, good. Doing the work isn't the problem. So, what happens when you go to turn it in?

The parent validates the parts of the situation that the child is doing correctly, while analyzing the specific aspects of the problem that she needs information on.

> *Child:* I don't know. I just don't turn it in.
>
> *Parent:* Hmm. What would happen if you did turn in your work?
>
> *Child:* I'd get good grades.
>
> *Parent:* And when you don't?
>
> *Child:* You know already—I fail my classes.
>
> *Parent:* And your friends, what kind of grades do they get?
>
> *Child:* Mixed.

TIP SHEET 16: DEALING WITH UNDERPERFORMANCE

✓ Try to determine the cause of the underperformance. Boredom and difficulties with peer status are common reasons.

✓ Work with the school to address the reasons.

✓ Brainstorm solutions with the child based on the cause of the underperformance.

✓ Be willing to be flexible and creative when developing a solution.

This whole section is fact finding. Simple, nonjudgmental questions designed to collect information helps the parent discover the reasons behind the behavior. Only then can a solution be found.

> *Parent:* How do they react when you get good grades?
>
> *Child:* Some of them call me a brainiac.

Now we are getting somewhere. Maybe the child doesn't like that. Maybe the kids he wants to hang out with are average students, or students who tend to fail. This is critically important information. The parent has done a good job here. From this point, the parent can coach the child into long-range planning and help point out any of the problems in the child's thinking. In situations like this one, the parent may need to deal with the problems of underperformance, commonly called underachievement. Tip Sheet 16 suggests ideas for parents to consider when dealing with underperformance in their gifted children.

NOTE TO THE TEACHER

Just as there are many opportunities to work with relationship issues between parents and children, there also are ample opportunities to work on these key issues within the school setting. Let's revisit the bullying scenario, changing the players to include a teacher and a gifted student.

SCENARIO

Your fifth-grade student tells you she is scared to go out to lunch because her best friend is being mean "all the time." This happens on the same day that the parent of the other student has e-mailed you with a concern that someone is bullying her at lunch. The other parent specifically named the student talking to you as being the student bullying her daughter and expects you to do something about it.

INITIAL TEACHER-CHILD DIALOGUE

> *Teacher:* Emma, is there anything going on between you and Shelly at lunch?
>
> *Student:* I don't want to talk about it.
>
> *Teacher:* I think we have to. You are telling me you are afraid to see her at lunch and she seems upset too.
>
> *Student:* It's no big deal. Can't I just stay in and help you with something? I hate going out to lunch anyways.
>
> *Teacher:* No, you have to go out to lunch. No one will be in the class, and I want you to work out whatever the problem is with Shelly. There is a problem, isn't there?
>
> *Student:* (Student begins to cry) There's nothing wrong.
>
> *Teacher:* Then why are you crying? Emma, you can either talk to me or we can go to the principal to talk about it.
>
> *Student:* (Student refuses to look at teacher and is still crying) I just don't feel good today. Nothing else is wrong. Can I have a pass to the nurse? I think I'm going to be sick.
>
> *Teacher:* You can have a pass, but I'm still going to have you talk

with the principal about this. You have to go to lunch. I can't have you two girls causing all this drama all the time.

Student: Fine. (Student walks out, deciding she can never speak about any of this with an adult ever again)

ANALYSIS OF DIALOGUE

In this scenario, Emma is having problems with her friend and no longer feels comfortable at school during more social activities (like lunch). The other child is involved, as her parent is already contacting the school for help. The dialogue that ensues does not move Emma toward a clear discussion of her feelings or result in a plan to deal with them. Instead, both the teacher and the student leave the conversation feeling powerless. Worse, the situation is not resolved and Emma feels as though there is no one to turn to on campus. With no clear understanding of the problem, none of the involved people can find resolution. Let's look at the specific problems with the dialogue.

Teacher: Emma, is there anything going on between you and Shelly at lunch?

Student: I don't want to talk about it.

Teacher: I think we have to. You are telling me you are afraid to see her at lunch and she seems upset too.

Student: It's no big deal. Can't I just stay in and help you with something? I hate going out to lunch anyways.

Teacher: No, you have to go out to lunch. No one will be in the class, and I want you to work out whatever the problem is with Shelly. There is a problem, isn't there?

Student: (Student begins to cry) There's nothing wrong.

Teacher: Then why are you crying? Emma, you can either talk to me or we can go to the principal to talk about it.

This initial phase of the exchange starts well. The teacher asks good questions and sets an appropriate boundary. Problems occur as the conversation pushes forward, and the student is placed in a highly defensive position. The conversation begins to deteriorate quickly at that point.

> *Student:* (Student refuses to look at teacher and is still crying) I just don't feel good today. Nothing else is wrong. Can I have a pass to the nurse? I think I'm going to be sick.
>
> *Teacher:* You can have a pass, but I'm still going to have you talk with the principal about this. You have to go to lunch. I can't have you two girls causing all this drama all the time.

Here, the teacher is stating an appropriate boundary. However, without knowing the actual dynamic of the problem, the teacher is pushing the student into a higher and higher state of defensiveness. The teacher has missed an opportunity to let the student talk with her about the problems and teach the student about the connection between her feelings and the friendship situation. Without the information such a conversation could deliver, the teacher cannot be certain as to whether or not actual bullying has occurred or the actual nature of the problem.

> *Student:* Fine. (Student walks out, deciding she can never speak about any of this with an adult ever again)

The student has ended the dialogue completely in this scenario—with nothing resolved and a bigger emotional concern.

New Dialogue Using Coaching Strategies

Using successful coaching techniques, as well as some of the strategies presented earlier in the book, let's see how this scenario can be improved.

> *Teacher:* Emma, is there anything going on between you and Shelly at lunch?
>
> *Student:* I don't want to talk about it.
>
> *Teacher:* You sound really upset Emma. Talking about it could really help.

Here the teacher is cueing Emma as to both her feelings and that it is "safe" to talk about it with her. If Emma has a strong enough emotional vocabulary, the cueing will be enough. If not, the teacher can continue cueing, making Emma feel safe to talk.

> *Student:* It's no big deal. Can't I just stay in and help you with something? I hate going out to lunch anyways.
>
> *Teacher:* Staying with me won't make any of the problems at lunch go away. But why don't you help me a little today and we can figure out what the problem is so you don't feel this way tomorrow.
>
> (The teacher does a good job giving the student a path toward a solution to the problem.)
>
> *Student:* (Student begins to cry) I can't talk about it. Really, there's nothing wrong.
>
> *Teacher:* (Teacher consoles student) Things won't get better if you hold it all inside. I know it's hard to talk sometimes, but you can trust me. Is it Shelly? Did you two get into an argument?

Assuming there is a good connection between the teacher and the student, Emma may be willing to disclose the problem at this point. If she is still unwilling, the teacher can use distraction by having the student help her with some other task and change the subject. After the student has calmed down, she can try asking about Shelly again. Typically, the student who wants to talk will do so at this point. Once the conversation begins, the teacher can help problem solve with Emma, without any of the drama.

If the child is not willing to talk, the teacher has a couple of options—let it all go and see what happens, inform the parents of the problem and see if they can solve it, or let another staff member try. In this case, I would advise informing the parents of the problem, while providing some strategies to help the parents resolve the issue.

We've gone through several of the more typical situations that come up in the area of relationships and peer interactions. In each of the scenarios, simple changes in the words we use when talking to our child, the tone of our voice, and the kinds of questions we ask can make all the difference in the word.

Next we'll go through situations related to gifted children and their performance in school.

CHAPTER 12
PERFORMANCE ISSUES

One of the key areas impacted by the emotional nature of giftedness is performance in school and other areas. Problems involving perfectionism, school achievement, resiliency and risk taking, and school-based phobias are born out of the emotional characteristics inherent in these children. Fortunately, those same characteristics also increase the effectiveness of various coaching strategies.

In this section, I will examine three of the more typical performance-based problems. Using the coaching and interventions strategies presented throughout this book, parent-child dialogue has the potential to positively impact your gifted child's ability to problem solve and regulate her own behavior.

PERFECTIONISM AND SCHOOL UNDERACHIEVEMENT

Gifted students often are perfectionists with regard to their schoolwork and extracurricular activities. Driven by a need to excel, they often believe that making a mistake means they are not smart, not capable, and somehow "wrong." They seldom see mistakes as a natural part of learning. As a result, gifted children typically get stuck by their need to do things perfectly. They may develop behaviors that look obsessive or refuse to turn in work that is not "perfect." Maybe they will spend

3 hours on an assignment that should only take 5 minutes, all because they were too scared they were doing it wrong. In this scenario, I will examine one of the more common ways perfectionist tendencies impact performance.

SCENARIO

Your 12-year-old child is refusing to turn in his schoolwork. As a result, the teacher has called home to inform you of the problem. After a little investigation, you have learned that your child has not turned in any of his schoolwork or homework in any of his classes. You have watched him complete the work, so you are at a loss as to what is going on.

INITIAL PARENT-CHILD DIALOGUE

> *Parent:* Vincent, I got a call from your teachers today. They said you haven't been turning in your work. What's going on? I know you're doing your work.
>
> *Child:* I turn it in Dad. The teacher just loses things. It happens to other kids too.
>
> *Parent:* I have a hard time believing that, Vincent. And I am really mad that you're lying to me now. Go to your room and don't come out until you're ready to tell me why you have been lying about your schoolwork.
>
> (Child storms off and slams his bedroom door, making the parent even more angry.)

ANALYSIS OF DIALOGUE

This scenario is very similar to the scenario with Eric in the last chapter. Like Eric, Vincent is completing his homework and not turning it in. However, Vincent's reasons for not turning in the work are very different—as is the dialogue between Vincent and his father. Although the father has set boundaries and expectations, he is easily angered and is not trying to determine the cause of his son's behavior. Let's take this apart line by line:

> *Parent:* Vincent, I got a call from your teachers today. They said you haven't been turning in your work. What's going on? I know you're doing your work.
>
> *Child:* I turn it in Dad. The teacher just loses things. It happens to other kids too.

The child's reaction is very typical, trying to refocus the attention away from himself and find someone else to blame.

> *Parent:* I have a hard time believing that, Vincent. And I am really mad that you're lying to me now. Go to your room and don't come out until you're ready to tell me why you have been lying about your schoolwork.

Unfortunately, the child has pushed his father's "mad" buttons. As a result, this dialogue immediately ends communication and extracts a punishment. No learning can take place. Furthermore, there is no way for either parent or child to determine the causes of the behavior or strategize a solution.

> (Child storms off and slams his bedroom door, making the parent even more angry)

Obviously this is a no-win situation. The child is not able to problem solve or determine other causes of his own behavior. In fact, this dialogue prohibits the child from even owning his behavioral choices.

NEW DIALOGUE USING
COACHING STRATEGIES

Using successful coaching techniques, as well as some of the strategies previously mentioned, this scenario can result in a positive learning
experience for everyone involved.

> *Parent:* Vincent, I got a call from your teachers today. They said you
> haven't been turning in your work. What's going on? I know
> you're doing your work.
>
> *Child:* I turn it in Dad. The teacher just loses things. It happens to
> other kids too.
>
> *Parent:* I am sorry about that happening to other kids, but let's fo-
> cus on you. You complete your work, correct?

The parent refocuses back to the child and begins fact-finding. The
next few exchanges will give the parent the information he needs to
know how to coach his son.

> *Child:* Yes.
>
> *Parent:* And when you get to class, do you know where to turn it in?
>
> *Child:* Of course Dad.

The parent ignores the sarcasm of the child and keeps the conversation on course.

> *Parent:* So, there seems to be a problem between you turning it in
> and the teacher recording it. Is that what you are saying?
>
> *Child:* (Remains quiet)
>
> *Parent:* Because I can go and talk to the teacher about this and we
> can help to search the classroom for your work.

At this point the parent believes his son likely did not turn it in. However, he wants to give his son an opportunity to admit the truth and discover the real problem.

> *Child:* Well, maybe I am forgetting to turn it in.

The parent does not respond angrily to this. This is important. You want to keep the child talking and parental anger would likely shut down the communication again.

> *Parent:* Oh, OK. Well, what do you think the problem is? Why aren't you able to turn in your work?
>
> *Child:* I don't know.

It is possible that the child really does not understand why he is behaving the way he is. This is when cueing and leading can help the parent lead the child to a discovery of the root cause of the behavior.

> *Parent:* Well, let's see if we can figure it out. You know, I used to not turn in work when I was afraid that it was wrong. Could that be happening to you sometimes?
>
> (Child remains quiet)
>
> *Parent:* Because if that is the problem, I think we can work on that.
>
> *Child:* That may be part of the problem Dad.

At this point, the parent can help the child understand how stress works and develop a solution to the negative feelings the child is trying to avoid by not turning in his work. Parents can use the suggestions in Tip Sheet 17 (see p. 162) to help their children overcome the sense of perfectionism many gifted children experience.

TIP SHEET 17: MANAGING PERFECTIONISM

✓ Teach the child to recognize and own his perfectionism.

✓ Guide the child in the development of realistic goals. Gifted children often take on more than they can do.

✓ Focus on the process, not the outcome, with your child.

✓ Teach your child to have a realistic view of things. Faulty perspective can lead to a deepening of the perfectionism concerns.

✓ Teach child to evaluate his behavior in terms of the following:

   » Is this realistic?

   » What would happen if I failed this?

   » Am I being realistic about this situation?

RESILIENCY AND RISK-TAKING

Achievement in school requires several skills, including persistence, the willingness to take a risk and step out of one's comfort zone, and the ability to bounce back after disappointment. Gifted children can struggle in any number of these areas related to the attributes of giftedness. Often these children are unfamiliar with the discomfort of taking academic risks and avoid that feeling at all costs. Or, because they seldom fail in their endeavors, they lack the resiliency necessary to help themselves overcome adversity. Either way, this is an area of difficulty for many gifted children.

Through strategic coaching and communication, parents can assist their children greatly, using challenging moments to teach new skills in this area.

The following scenario presents one way in which children struggle when faced with the unusual feeling of being unsuccessful.

Scenario

Your 10-year-old child is an Olympic-bound swimmer. He works very hard every day to meet his time standards. And as a result, he has been placed in a very competitive level of swimming. His coach explains that he will need to work very hard to maintain the level of swimming required to remain in the group. Your child gets nervous, but attempts to meet the coach's demands.

One day, the practice is particularly hard, working on skills with which your child is unfamiliar. He struggles to complete the practice and requires additional breaks. This has never happened before, causing your son some distress. At the end of practice, your son tells you he doesn't like to swim anymore and would rather try a different sport.

Initial Parent-Child Dialogue

Parent: John, are you sure you want to switch sports? You just moved into this level.

Child: Yeah, I'm sure. I am tired of swimming and I need a change.

Parent: Does this have anything to do with practice tonight?

Child: Not really, I just need a change.

Parent: Well OK, but you can switch only after the month is over. After all, we paid for it and you made a commitment.

(The next day, the child still refuses to go to practice)

Child: Mom, I can't go to practice. I have too much work to do.

Parent: Now John, you promised. We have to go.

Child: I told you I don't want to swim anymore. I'm not going. (Child's voice gets angry and he walks out of the room and slams the door)

ANALYSIS OF DIALOGUE

In this scenario, John is struggling with his new swim expectations. He has found a way out of the problem that seems responsible and he is able to communicate it relatively well with the parent. The problem comes in the long-term impact of the conversation—either John will be allowed to stop swimming when he is afraid, sending a dangerous message for future endeavors, or Mom has to force him to attend, resulting in a big scene at the pool. Either way, the core problem of John's fear and his need to be "right" or "the best" won't be addressed. Let's look at the specific problems with the dialogue.

> *Parent:* John, are you sure you want to switch sports? You just moved into this level.
>
> *Child:* Yeah, I'm sure. I am tired of swimming and I need a change.
>
> *Parent:* Does this have anything to do with practice tonight?

The parent has done a good job with asking the question. However, by posing it in a yes/no format it almost guarantees a "no" and prevents any additional dialogue on the subject.

> *Child:* Not really, I just need a change.
>
> *Parent:* Well OK, but you can switch only after the month is over. After all, we paid for it and you made a commitment.
>
> (The next day, the child still refuses to go to practice)
>
> *Child:* Mom, I can't go to practice. I have too much work to do.
>
> *Parent:* Now John, you promised. We have to go.
>
> *Child:* I told you I don't want to swim anymore. I'm not going. (Child's voice gets angry and he walks out of the room and slams the door)

Although the dialogue in and of itself is not the problem, the situation is. The parent has placed both the child and herself in a no-win situation, and John will not learn anything from this.

NEW DIALOGUE USING COACHING STRATEGIES

Using successful coaching techniques, as well as some of the strategies previously mentioned, let's see how this scenario can be improved.

> *Parent:* John, are you sure you want to switch sports? You just moved into this level.
>
> *Child:* Yeah, I'm sure. I am tired of swimming and I need a change.
>
> *Parent:* I understand that. I'll tell you what, after you have overcome your difficulties in this level, we can switch sports.

Here the parent is identifying the problem early. The child *will* have a reaction—likely negative—to this, but let's see what happens.

> *Child:* What problems? I just need a change.
>
> *Parent:* John, I watched you struggle with the practice today, and I know you don't usually struggle.
>
> *Child:* Yeah, but that has nothing to do with it. I just want to try something new.
>
> *Parent:* And you are welcome to switch sports when this is no longer about something being hard.

The parent is setting a difficult boundary and expectation. The child will have some poor reactions initially.

Parent: John, let's talk with your coach and get in some extra swim time for another 2 weeks. If things are better after that, great. If not, we can discuss our options at that point. The key is to not give up when it gets hard.

If the child is open to the conversation at this point, the parent can use it as a teachable moment to explain or reinforce how our minds will try to convince us something is unachievable when that may not be true. This then becomes an opportunity to learn how to face adversity with a plan to overcome it and move forward.

One of the important aspects with this scenario is the need to coach, cue, and teach your child ways to overcome adversity and build resiliency. Gifted children can be very hesitant in this regard, so strategic teaching often is necessary. Tip Sheet 18, on page 167, provides some suggestions for parents in teaching their children how to develop resiliency.

SCHOOL-BASED PHOBIAS

Occasionally, the anxiety produced by the pressure to perform well in school can rise to the level of paralysis—situations in which the child is completely unable to function in a traditional learning situation. With gifted children and the nature of their emotional development, this can happen somewhat frequently. And, although the behavior is somewhat scary to deal with, it does not necessarily mean there is a mental illness issue with the child.

Coaching and behavioral interventions often are all that is required to make a significant positive impact on the emotional functioning of the child. Take this scenario of a child who has stopped coming to school.

TIP SHEET 18: DEVELOPING RESILIENCY

✓ Help your child know how to be a good friend.

✓ Teach your child to give back.

✓ Establish healthy habits and routines.

✓ Teach your child to take time for breaks.

✓ Teach your child to set goals, but remain flexible with them.

✓ Teach your child to be an optimist by focusing on what works in a situation first.

Scenario

Your 13-year-old child gets up and gets ready for school. However, when it is time to leave, she begins to cry and throws a temper tantrum. This continues many times a week. When you are able to get the child to school, she often calls to go home within the first hour.

This particular morning you managed to get her into the car. But now that you are at school, she won't get out.

Initial Parent-Child Dialogue

Parent: Gabriella, you have to go to school. I'm late for work and I can't keep doing this with you.

Child: (Begins to cry again) But Mom, I can't go. I just can't.

Parent: It isn't a choice. Get out of the car.

Child: (Cries even harder) No, Mommy. I really can't go in there.

Parent: Gabby, stop it. Get out of this car before I drag you out.

Child: No! (The crying is loud and intense)

Parent: (Frustrated and powerless, the parent acquiesces) Fine. I'll let you stay at home today. But this is the last time, Gabby. I

> can't afford to lose my job because of this. You have to go to
> school.

ANALYSIS OF DIALOGUE

Gabriella is clearly struggling to attend school. Her parent is at a loss as to how to help. She tries consoling, bribing, and threatening her daughter—all with no discernible positive outcome. Finally she gives up. Unfortunately, that only makes things worse. Let's look and see where the exact problems are so we can create a better dialogue.

> *Parent:* Gabriella, you have to go to school. I'm late for work and I
>   can't keep doing this with you.
> *Child:* (Begins to cry again) But Mom, I can't go. I just can't.
> *Parent:* It isn't a choice. Get out of the car.

The parent does a good job of setting both the expectation and the boundary. However, by forcing her before she is ready, she is forcing the child into a flight or fight mode. Gifted children, in particular, snap into this easily. And once this happens, their ability to reason logically evaporates.

> *Child:* (Cries even harder) No, Mommy. I really can't go in there.
> *Parent:* Gabby, stop it. Get out of this car before I drag you out.

Now the parent has made a threat out of frustration—something she is likely not going to follow through on. This can create even more problems and the power the child now wields to control her parent's emotions becomes addicting to the child.

> *Child:* No! (The crying is loud and intense)

> *Parent:* (Frustrated and powerless, the parent acquiesces) Fine. I'll let you stay at home today. But this is the last time, Gabby. I can't afford to lose my job because of this. You have to go to school.

The child's ultimate manipulation has worked and the child has gotten what she was after. This will perpetuate a cycle that will get more and more difficult to solve every time it is allowed to happen.

New Dialogue Using Coaching Strategies

Using successful coaching techniques, as well as some of the strategies previously mentioned, this scenario can have a much different ending. Let's look at one possible outcome.

> *Parent:* Gabriella, you have to go to school. You may either walk to class on your own, or we can get some help from the office.

The boundaries and expectations are set, but this time the child is given some choice in the outcome.

> *Child:* (Begins to cry again) But Mommy, I can't go. I just can't.
>
> *Parent:* I know this is difficult for you. But we only have two options, go by yourself to class, or get assistance from the office. Which one would you like to do?

The delivery of this line is critically important. There should be little to no emotional response at this point. Furthermore, as the child escalates to the point of a temper tantrum (something that will likely occur), the parent needs to remain calm and simply repeat the options.

> *Child:* (Cries even harder) No, Mommy. I really can't go in there.
>
> *Parent:* (Remain calm) I know you can do this. Would you like to go to class by yourself or would you like to go to the office?

The child often will increase the intensity of the temper tantrum to get you to comply. However, if you remain calm and nonemotional and continue to offer the two choices, the child typically will give up and go to class.

Sometimes, the problem is a little more severe. In that case, enlisting the help of the administration or counseling staff at the school can be wonderful. In that situation, after a couple of times of offering your child the choice to go to class or the office, the parent would then make the decision for the child as follows:

> *Parent:* I can see this is really hard for you. So, we are going to go inside and talk with someone.
>
> *Child:* No! I won't go in there.
>
> *Parent:* Let's just try.

At this point the child usually will go in. If not, it is OK to get someone to come out and help take the child inside the office. The key is to get the child through the front door of the school.

Once inside, the parent can let the office know the situation. Many times a counselor, administrator, or other support staff member can take the child. At that point it is important for the parent to leave. More often than not, once the parent has left and the child realizes there is no choice in the matter, she will go to school.

At the end of the day, the parent should follow up with the child and begin the process of determining why the child was struggling to begin with. Performance issues and anxiety often are the cause of this type of scenario. The techniques outlined in Chapter 8, especially the Proof

●← TIP SHEET 19: REDUCING SOCIAL AND SCHOOL ANXIETY

✓ Help your child develop healthy habits with regard to sleeping, eating, and exercise.

✓ Teach relaxation techniques to your child.

✓ Practice positive self-talk with your child.

✓ Work on a child's perspective, reminding her that nothing is ever all good or all bad. Teach your child to be realistic in his view of life.

✓ Mental Rehearsal can help if the anxiety is preventing performance on a specific task.

strategy, can be very helpful in redirecting a gifted child and teaching her to discern false mental messages she may be holding.

It may take a while to redirect school phobia (see Tip Sheet 19, on p. 171, for advice on reducing social and school anxiety). Getting the child to school is really only a part of the issue. Long-lasting results require the enlistment of knowledgeable school personnel or counselors to help the child understand how to redirect her thinking so that school no longer is the focus of her stress.

NOTES TO THE TEACHER

School-based problems are ideal situations to try to utilize positive coaching strategies with teachers and students. Let's take the initial scenario presented in this chapter—the gifted child who is not turning in his classwork—and change the players to include a teacher and the child.

SCENARIO

One of your gifted students in your sixth-grade class is not turning in his homework. Even classwork is seldom turned in. You have called home to inform the parents of the problem. They assure you that the student is doing all of the work and that they are checking his daily planner every night. The parents are at a loss at this point, as are you. You decide the only way to get at the heart of the problem is to confront the student about the lack of work being turned in.

INITIAL PARENT-CHILD DIALOGUE

Teacher: Vincent, I am very concerned about your progress in class. You have not turned in your last four homework assignments and your classwork is incomplete. I spoke with your parents and they assured me that you are doing the work at home. What is going on? Why aren't you turning in the work?

Student: I do turn it in. I don't know why you don't have it.

Teacher: Vincent, we both know that isn't true. If you are saying I am the reason I have no grades for you, this is a problem. If you have turned in the assignments, I would have grades and I would have returned them to you. Do you have the graded work?

Student: No. I don't keep that stuff. But I know I'm turning it in.

Teacher: I don't have it, so you are NOT turning it in. Your grades at this point will be lowered because of the missing assignments. You have to start turning in your things.

Student: (Student is visibly angry) Is that all?

Teacher: Yes.

(Student leaves without another word)

ANALYSIS OF DIALOGUE

This scenario is very similar to the scenario with Eric in the last chapter. Like Eric, Vincent is completing his homework and not turning it in. However, Vincent's reasons for not turning in the work are very different—as is the dialogue between Vincent and his teacher. Although the teacher is setting appropriate boundaries and stating expectations and consequences, his frustration with Vincent is apparent and he is utilizing a more authoritative demeanor. The result? Neither the teacher, nor the parents really know why Vincent is refusing to turn in work. Furthermore, Vincent appears unwilling to provide such answers at this point. Let's look at the actual dialogue a bit closer:

> *Teacher:* Vincent, I am very concerned about your progress in class. You have not turned in your last four homework assignments and your classwork is incomplete. I spoke with your parents and they assured me that you are doing the work at home. What is going on? Why aren't you turning in the work?
>
> *Student:* I do turn it in. I don't know why you don't have it.

Blaming the teacher or another person is typical for students, especially for those at Vincent's age. The trick is to find a way to elicit the truth.

> *Teacher:* Vincent, we both know that isn't true. If you are saying I am the reason I have no grades for you, this is a problem. If you have turned in the assignments, I would have grades and I would have returned them to you. Do you have the graded work?
>
> *Student:* No. I don't keep that stuff. But I know I'm turning it in.
>
> *Teacher:* I don't have it, so you are NOT turning it in. Your grades at this point will be lowered because of the missing assignments. You have to start turning in your things.

Unfortunately, the teacher has slipped into authoritative mode, instead of coaching mode. As this happens, the teacher has become more concerned with establishing boundaries and expectations (not necessarily a bad thing) rather than using the moment to discover why the problem is happening in the first place. A teachable moment is lost as both parties push to be seen as correct.

> *Student:* (Student is visibly angry) Is that all?
>
> *Teacher:* Yes.
>
> (Student leaves without another word)

Obviously this is a no-win situation. The teacher has no solution to Vincent not turning in his work and Vincent leaves the conversation with no admission of the problem and no solution. An opportunity to learn an important lesson is lost as the teacher and student both get stuck in their own emotions.

NEW DIALOGUE USING COACHING STRATEGIES

Using successful coaching techniques, as well as some of the strategies previously mentioned, this scenario can result in a positive learning experience for everyone involved.

> *Teacher:* Vincent, I am very concerned about your progress in class. You have not turned in your last four homework assignments and your classwork is incomplete. I spoke with your parents and they assured me that you are doing the work at home. What is going on? Why aren't you turning in the work?
>
> *Student:* I do turn it in. I don't know why you don't have it.
>
> *Teacher:* I typically don't lose student work, but maybe we should

> look through the papers that need to be given back to see if
> any of it is there. Also, you can check your work at home to
> see if you have it. If you do, I am more than happy to change
> the grade. You are completing the work and turning it in, right?

The teacher does a good job of refocusing the conversation back without stating that the student is lying. He also gives the student a way to see if this is a teacher or student problem. The next few exchanges should give the teacher even more information as to what the core problem may be.

> *Student:* Yes, I do most of the work.
>
> *Teacher:* On the work you complete, do you know where and when to turn it in?
>
> *Student:* Yes.
>
> *Teacher:* And on the work you don't turn in, is it because you are not sure of the instructions or something else?
>
> *Student:* (Silent and looking away)
>
> (The teacher ignores the silence and continues)
>
> *Teacher:* So, it seems that maybe the assignments are unclear. At least on the ones you don't complete. (The teacher waits for a response)
>
> *Student:* (After a long silence) Sometimes I am not certain what to do.

At this point the teacher can get to the truth of the problem and develop a game plan.

> *Teacher:* OK, at those times, how can you figure out what to do?
>
> *Student:* I can call a friend.

> *Teacher:* That's a great idea. Can you think of anything else you can do?

Now the teacher and student are working together to find a solution to the student's problem of not understanding the assignment. Once a game plan for understanding the assignment is figured out, the teacher can move to other aspects of the problem.

> *Teacher:* Now, about the things you said you have turned in, but I have not recorded. Can you look through your work at home and bring in the work that you may have?

The teacher is fairly certain the student was not completely honest about this, but by acknowledging the student, he is able to help the student learn another important lesson.

> *Student:* Well, I don't keep the work.
>
> *Teacher:* Hmm. That is a problem. I can only change the zero to a grade if I know what the grade was.
>
> (Again the teacher is not calling the student out, merely pointing out a problem with not keeping work)
>
> *Teacher:* For now, go through anything you have and bring it to me to check against my records. In the future, keep all graded work for the entire grading period, just in case a teacher makes a mistake. OK?
>
> *Student:* Yeah, OK.

The conversation ends on a positive note with the student having learned ways to deal with work he does not understand and how to ensure he gets proper credit for anything he completes—both important lessons to learn. The teacher can now inform the parent of the outcome and everyone can follow up to see that a positive change will actually result.

We've gone through several of the more typical situations that come up in the area of performance. In each of the scenarios, most of the communication by the parents was appropriate. However, none of the initial dialogues concentrated on problem solving or teaching. This is the biggest difference between coaching your child and traditional parenting—a shift from managing a problem to teaching the child how to problem solve and manage his own behaviors.

Next we'll go through various types of behavior and discipline issues.

CHAPTER 13
BEHAVIOR

Gifted children are subject to the same kind of behavioral difficulties as their nongifted counterparts. However, working with their behavioral challenges requires more than simple reward and consequence techniques. Often, it requires a good understanding of the communication aspects of behavior.

Most children behave as they do to communicate a need to get something, escape something, or protest. Through role-plays of various scenarios, a parent can learn the strategies necessary to diffuse behavior problems, understand what need the child was attempting to communicate, and help shape a new, more appropriate way to get that need met.

INTERNAL BEHAVIORS

Internalized behaviors are those behaviors that result from a child taking in the stressors of his world and turning his frustration inward. Often born out of a need to escape, these behaviors include withdrawal, depression, and anxiety. School phobias, performance-related issues, and poor peer interactions all can be related to an internalization of behavior.

In the following scenario, internalized behaviors are handled through a mixture of positive coaching and communication.

Scenario

Your child has a writing exam in her language arts class. Before the test, she goes to the nurse complaining of a stomachache. She calls you and asks to come home. You agree to get her, as the flu has been going around. Once home, you daughter has no indicators of a stomachache or anything else.

Initial Parent-Child Dialogue

> *Parent:* Katie, I think we need to talk about today? Why did you ask to come home?
>
> *Child:* My stomach hurt and I felt like I was going to throw up.
>
> *Parent:* Was this before or after your writing test?
>
> *Child:* Just before. But really, Mom, my stomach did hurt. And I did need to come home.
>
> *Parent:* And since you've been home, has your stomach ached at all?
>
> *Child:* (Child pauses for a minute) No, I guess not. But it did hurt before.
>
> *Parent:* Well, next time you have to stay at school.
>
> (Child cries and nods)

This cycle repeats itself on the next couple of writing tests.

Analysis of Dialogue

In this scenario, Katie is demonstrating significant anxiety, likely related to the testing situation. She internalizes the stressors and displays a physical reaction to them. The conversation, although appropriate, failed to help Katie identify the actual problem or her behavioral response, and a new way to respond to the problem. In short, there was a missed opportunity to teach Katie how to self-monitor her feelings, and adjust her behavior. The result is a pattern of response that is repeated over and over again. Let's look at the how this was created within the specific dialogue:

> *Parent:* Katie, I think we need to talk about today? Why did you ask to come home?
>
> *Child:* My stomach hurt and I felt like I was going to throw up.
>
> *Parent:* Was this before or after your writing test?

This is a good beginning as the parent clearly is trying to ascertain the exact function of the behavior her daughter is demonstrating.

> *Child:* Just before. But really, Mom, my stomach did hurt. And I did need to come home.
>
> *Parent:* And since you've been home, has your stomach ached at all?
>
> *Child:* (Child pauses for a minute) No, I guess not. But it did hurt before.
>
> *Parent:* Well, next time you have to stay at school.

Most of this exchange is strong. However, when the parent set the boundary, open communication was ended. There are no opportunities to discuss the exact reason, or function, of the behavior.

> (Child cries and nods)

Overall, this conversation demonstrates a failure to make use of the teachable moment to effectively determine the nature of the child's behaviors.

NEW DIALOGUE USING
COACHING STRATEGIES

Using successful coaching techniques, as well as some of the strategies presented earlier in the book, let's see how this scenario can be improved.

> *Parent:* Katie, you had a rough day today. Why did you ask to come home?

This is a little more direct than the first example.

> *Child:* My stomach hurt and I felt like I was going to throw up.
>
> *Parent:* Was this before or after your writing test?

This is good, as the parent is establishing a timeline and connection for the behavior.

> *Child:* Just before. But really, Mom, my stomach did hurt. And I did need to come home.
>
> *Parent:* And since you've been home, has your stomach ached at all?
>
> *Child:* (Child pauses for a minute) No, I guess not. But it did hurt before.
>
> *Parent:* I'm sure it did. Sometimes our stomach hurts when we get upset or nervous. Could you have been nervous?

Here the parent is trying to walk the child through an analysis of her behavior.

> *Child:* I don't know. It just hurt.
>
> *Parent:* If you did know, what do you think your answer would be?

**⊶ TIP SHEET 20: HELPING
CHILDREN DEAL WITH STRESS**

✓ Make sure children get plenty of rest.

✓ Create a calm environment at home.

✓ Teach children to practice yoga, meditation, or other forms of deep relaxation. Make this a regular part of the routine at home.

✓ Establish effective communication between parents and children.

This trick works with many children, helping them move past the "I don't know" response and to the actual feelings.

> *Child:* I guess that I was a little nervous. Maybe.
>
> *Parent:* OK, well what could you do the next time you feel nervous?

The parent has now opened the door to try the various techniques outlined in Chapters 7 and 8. These techniques, coupled with improved communication skills, can turn this repeated behavior into a teachable moment—one that could lay the foundation for working through all stressful situations. Tip Sheet 20 suggests additional strategies for helping children deal with stress.

EXTERNAL BEHAVIORS

Just as internal behaviors deal with those behaviors that are turned inward, external behaviors refer to acting-out behaviors, including most forms of aggression (verbal and physical outbursts), tantrums, and rage.

SCENARIO

Your 15-year-old child frequently throws things around in her bedroom when she is stressed or tired. Additionally, she yells, pounds her fists on the walls, and slams her door. You have tried traditional discipline, like time out and grounding as a way of dealing with the problems. You have even tried more physical forms of discipline. But nothing seems to help deter the behavior.

This particular scenario happened in response to the parent hearing her daughter throw things around her room after school one day.

INITIAL PARENT-CHILD DIALOGUE

> *Parent:* Lisa, you need to stop destroying your room. This isn't the way to handle your frustration.
>
> *Child:* (Begins to cry) I know Mom. But I can't help it. I get too frustrated.
>
> *Parent:* I know that. But you need to learn to control your temper. What would your teachers think if they saw you doing this?
>
> *Child:* But you don't understand. (Child cries harder and begins to pick at her skin)
>
> *Parent:* You're right, Lisa, I don't—I don't know why you think things are so hard. You have a good family, good friends, and earn good grades. There is no reason for all of this drama. (Parent's voice indicates frustration)
>
> *Child:* It isn't about that. And I don't want to talk about this anymore. (Child storms off, still crying)
>
> *Parent:* Lisa! Lisa! (Parent goes after child and argument ensues, escalating to a yelling match)

Analysis of Dialogue

In this scenario, Lisa is earning good grades and follows most school rules. However, she has a strong temper, often taking out her frustration on property or her parents. She does not handle conflict or confrontation well. As a result, any attempt by the parent to discuss the situation results in a yelling match.

The dialogue in this scenario begins without a problem. However, it quickly disintegrates, resulting in a no-win situation for both Lisa and her mother. Let's look at this more closely.

> *Parent:* Lisa, you need to stop destroying your room. This isn't the way to handle your frustration.

This is not a bad way to start. However, it can easily be misunderstood by the child as a direct confrontation—something guaranteed to end poorly in the long run.

> *Child:* (Begins to cry) I know Mom. But I can't help it. I get too frustrated.

The child resorts to crying as a result of the frustration. Nevertheless, she does communicate the problem clearly at this point.

> *Parent:* I know that. But you need to learn to control your temper. What would your teachers think if they saw you doing this?

This dialogue works only to shame the child, instead of seeking answers regarding the frustration.

> *Child:* But you don't understand. (Child cries harder and begins to pick at her skin)

From the child's perspective, there is no point in continuing the conversation, as she is not being heard.

> *Parent:* You're right Lisa, I don't—I don't know why you think things are so hard. You have a good family, good friends, and earn good grades. There is no reason for all of this drama. (Parent's voice indicates frustration)

Obviously nothing good is going to happen at this point. The parent is very frustrated and that feeling has blocked any ability to redirect the conversation into a problem-solving dialogue. At this point, it would be better for the parent to simply walk away and reinitiate once she is less frustrated.

> *Child:* It isn't about that. And I don't want to talk about this any-more. (Child storms off, still crying)
>
> *Parent:* Lisa! Lisa! (Parent goes after child and argument ensues, escalating to a yelling match)

Again, this obviously is the wrong move to make. Faced with a child who is unwilling to work out her frustration, the parent should just let her daughter go and calm down. Instead, the engagement leads to a bigger problem.

New Dialogue Using Coaching Strategies

Using successful coaching techniques, as well as some of the strategies previously mentioned, this scenario can be resolved with a much improved outcome.

> *Parent:* Lisa, you seem really frustrated. What's going on?

This beginning is less confrontational than the previous one.

> *Child:* (Begins to cry) I don't know, Mom. I'm just really frustrated.
>
> *Parent:* I'm sorry sweetie. Is there anything in particular that is frustrating? Or is it just the amount of things you have going on?

Offering a choice of responses is a good way to start this line of questioning. Often gifted children struggle when things are too open ended, stressing over the accuracy of their response. This type of questioning helps prevent that by offering a clear way to begin the conversation.

> *Child:* I don't know. It just seems like everyone is mad at me all the time. And everything I do is wrong—all of the time.

The child's answers give clues as to nature of her frustration. In this example, her perception is one of failure, despite the numerous successes she has had.

> *Parent:* Things can feel that way sometimes. But I think maybe your mind is telling you things that aren't true, like "people are mad at you" and what not. Remember when we talked about how a bright mind like yours can sometimes get things wrong?

Here the parent validates the feelings, provides an alternate explanation for what she may be experiencing, and recalls past conversations on the topic, in hopes of leading the child to the discover the tools in her emotional toolbox appropriate to deal with the problem.

 TIP SHEET 21: DIFFUSING ANGER

Teach your child the following strategies to help diffuse his or her frustration and anger:

- ✓ Know your triggers.
- ✓ Take a deep breath.
- ✓ Count to 10.
- ✓ Walk away.
- ✓ Find a safe person you can always vent to when you are angry.

Child: Yeah, but it really seems like people are mad.

From this point the parent can direct the conversation to help the child use the emotional vocabulary she has previously learned and seek a resolution. It is a stronger outcome that can give the child lifelong skills needed to overcome the child's temper. Other suggestions for diffusing a child's angry outbursts can be found in Tip Sheet 21.

RISKY BEHAVIORS

The teen years are a scary time for every parent. More and more our children are confronted with all sorts of situations and risky behaviors— drugs, alcohol, and self-injurious behaviors. Knowing how to handle these situations is the key to navigating through these difficult years. Gifted children, despite their strong cognitive skills, are not immune to these difficulties. In fact, their need to fit in can negatively impact their decision-making processes as they move through the teen years.

Fortunately, role-playing and talking openly about these situations can lead to healthy choices.

SCENARIO

Your child is invited to a party. You are concerned about drugs and alcohol at the party. This conversation is one attempt at discussing this scary topic before the child attends the party.

INITIAL PARENT-CHILD DIALOGUE

Parent: Tomas, your mother told me you are going to a party with Jaime tonight.

Child: Yeah. After the game.

Parent: Now son, I was young once. I remember . . .

Child: Dad, seriously, this isn't the sex speech is it? (Child is laughing)

Parent: (Embarrassed) Um . . . no. Actually this is the drugs and alcohol talk. What do you know about the friends throwing the party? I mean, I don't want you there if there are no parents, no . . .

Child: Dad, relax. John said his parents are going to be there. And even if there are drugs or whatever, don't assume I'm taking them. Look, Mom already said I can go. So, I'm going. (Child leaves, and parent is left feeling isolated)

ANALYSIS OF DIALOGUE

In this scenario, Tomas is going to a party. His father is concerned about the big three—sex, drugs, and alcohol. He initiates a conversation with his son, but it is awkward, and his son winds up leading the conversation. Tomas ends the communication before his father is ready, resulting in feelings of isolation. A couple of small changes could have a dramatic impact on the conversation. Let's take a look:

> *Parent:* Tomas, your mother told me you are going to a party with Jaime tonight.
>
> *Child:* Yeah. After the game.
>
> *Parent:* Now son, I was young once. I remember . . .

The parent is trying to build a connection, but it comes off sounding both unauthentic and awkward.

> *Child:* Dad, seriously, this isn't the sex speech is it? (Child is laughing)

The son is clearly not interested in "the talk," sensing his parent's awkwardness with the subject matter.

> *Parent:* (Embarrassed) Um . . . no. Actually this is the drugs and alcohol talk. What do you know about the friends throwing the party? I mean, I don't want you there if there are no parents, no . . .

Again, the parent is clearly uncomfortable and grasping at straws. The word choice is fine, but there is a lot behind the words that leads to uncomfortable feelings.

> *Child:* Dad, relax. John said his parents are going to be there. And even if there are drugs or whatever, don't assume I'm taking them. Look, Mom already said I can go. So, I'm going. (Child leaves, and parent is left feeling isolated)

The son has effectively ended the conversation—long before the parent was ready. The result? The parent feels like he was not heard.

NEW DIALOGUE USING COACHING STRATEGIES

Using successful coaching techniques, as well as some of the strategies previously mentioned, this scenario can result in less awkward moments, despite the content.

> *Parent:* Tomas, your mother told me you are going to a party with Jaime tonight.
>
> *Child:* Yeah. After the game.
>
> *Parent:* Sounds fun. I assume you checked to make sure the parents will be home?

The parent is reminding the child of the rules—the expectation of parental supervision. This exchange assumes trust between the parent and child. If the trust was missing, this is a phone call the child would make with the parent present.

> *Child:* Of course. Only way Mom would agree.
>
> *Parent:* And you've thought about the whole drug and alcohol thing?

This is reminding the child of the previous conversations the family has had regarding risky behaviors and reminding the child about the expectations. Again, this presumes a prior conversation on this topic. It is important to deal with these types of issues before the child is confronted with it.

> *Child:* Dad, relax. I've thought about all of this. You know my feelings about drugs.
>
> *Parent:* Yes. And I also remember what it's like to be your age. Just

TIP SHEET 22: TALKING ABOUT THE BIG THREE: SEX, ALCOHOL, AND DRUGS

✓ Don't wait for your child to come to you with questions.

✓ Start early. Speak often.

✓ Create an open and safe environment with your child.

✓ Clearly communicate values.

✓ Be open and honest.

✓ Listen actively to your child.

think before you act, OK? On the drugs, the drinking, and the sex . . . all of it. OK?

The parent is not afraid to openly discuss typical behaviors that occur at teen parties. His open manner makes the conversation more comfortable for the child. The previous conversations on this topic also establish open lines of communication on these important topics.

Child: Yeah, OK, Dad. Thanks.

In the end, the parent was able to bring the previous conversations regarding risky behaviors to the forefront of the child's mind. This will not guarantee that the child engages in appropriate behavior all the time, but it will minimize the risks. If you have not had conversations about risky behaviors with your child, and you feel the timing is appropriate to do so, you can use the suggestions in Tip Sheet 22 to aid you in your conversation.

NOTES TO THE TEACHER

Perhaps the most difficult behavior to work with in a traditional classroom setting is aggressive, externalized behaviors—things like throwing classwork on the ground or yelling out in class. When these behaviors are conducted by typical students, the authoritative and punitive approach usually taken will work. However, most kids do better when a little time is taken to look at the reason for the behaviors in the first place.

This is particularly true when working with gifted or dually exceptional children. Let's revisit the externalized behaviors scenario, changing it a bit to reflect the type of external aggressive behavior often seen in the classroom setting, especially when dealing with dually exceptional gifted children.

Scenario

You have a 12-year-old student who is both gifted and diagnosed with autism spectrum disorder in your class. The student is very high functioning and requires few accommodations to the curriculum. She is highly verbal and can typically understand all directions in class. However, she does get overwhelmed and begins to physically act out in class. When this happens, she may throw her things onto the floor or kick the students around her. You have tried traditional disciplinary strategies, like sending her out of the class or sending her to the principal. At the suggestion of the school psychologist, you even tried to make the work a bit easier for the student. However, these approaches seem to make the matter worse as the student seems to escalate in class with greater frequency, making it hard to teach the rest of the students in class.

This particular scenario happened in response to a request for work from the instructional assistant to the student.

INITIAL TEACHER-STUDENT DIALOGUE

> *Teacher:* Alana, you need to stop throwing your classwork on the floor. This isn't how we handle being frustrated.
>
> *Student:* (Cries and throws more paper from her desk to the floor) I know. I know. Too hard.
>
> *Teacher:* Alana, this is the same work you did yesterday. It isn't too hard. Now stop throwing things and get to work.
>
> *Student:* Can't. Too hard. (Student rocks back and forth, pulling at the hairs on her arm)
>
> *Teacher:* Alana. You have to stop. You don't see any of the other students throwing things, do you?
>
> (Student escalates further until teacher has to call for assistance)

ANALYSIS OF DIALOGUE

In this scenario, Alana is doing well in her classes and can usually maintain her behavior. However, she is stubborn and strong-willed. When she gets frustrated, she has few skills to handle the frustration and typically begins to throw things. Her usually large vocabulary gets reduced to simple utterances. Although her teacher is trained on the unique needs of gifted students and students with autism, she has never had a dually exceptional child in her class before. As a result, some of her strategies have proven ineffective in dealing with Alana.

The dialogue in this scenario disintegrates quickly, resulting in the need for outside assistance and an interruption to learning in the classroom. Let's look at this more closely.

> *Teacher:* Alana, you need to stop throwing your classwork on the floor. This isn't how we handle being frustrated.

This is not a bad way to start. But the tone and word choice can be overwhelming to the child. In this type of scenario, a low-key approach with minimal language would be better.

> *Student:* (Cries and throws more paper from her desk to the floor) I know. I know. Too hard.
>
> *Teacher:* Alana, this is the same work you did yesterday. It isn't too hard. Now stop throwing things and get to work.
>
> *Student:* Can't. Too hard. (Student rocks back and forth, pulling at the hairs on her arm)

This dialogue works only to shame the child further and does nothing to reduce the stress to the child.

> *Teacher:* Alana. You have to stop. You don't see any of the other students throwing things, do you?
>
> (Student escalates further until teacher has to call for assistance)

Obviously nothing good is going to happen at this point. The teacher and student are both too frustrated, blocking any possibility of having this end with a solution. At this point, it would be better for the student to be removed to a quiet location and the teacher to regain control of her class.

NEW DIALOGUE USING COACHING STRATEGIES

Using successful coaching techniques, as well as some of the strategies previously mentioned, this scenario can be resolved with a much improved outcome. It is important to note that a good outcome in this scenario is enhanced when the teacher is given information and training with regards to both giftedness and working with students with autism.

> *Teacher:* Alana, you seem really frustrated. What's going on?

This beginning is less confrontational than the previous one.

> *Student:* (Cries but does not throw anything else) Too hard. Too hard.
>
> *Teacher:* What's too hard, Alana? Show me.

Asking Alana to show her what is wrong is a great way to begin to find out the actual problem. With dually exceptional children, the actual problem is seldom what it seems to be initially. Furthermore, both gifted children and students with autism struggle when things are too open ended, stressing over the accuracy of their response. This type of questioning helps prevent that by offering a clear way to begin the conversation.

> *Student:* Too hard. Too hard. (Student points to worksheet on her desk)
>
> *Teacher:* Is the work too hard? Or is it confusing?

By offering a choice, the student can begin the conversation without getting hung up on trying to figure out where to begin.

> *Student:* Worksheet is too hard.

At this point, the teacher knows the apparent source of the student's discomfort and can make a decision whether or not to continue with the assignment or offer an alternative assignment.

> *Teacher:* OK, Alana. Look through your choice file and pick something else.

(A file was previously established for these moments)

Teacher: After you have something picked, get back to work. OK?

Student: (Calms down and grabs choice folder) OK.

From this point the teacher can continue with the lesson. After the student completes the worksheet, the teacher or instructional assistant can review with Alana how to ask for help and debrief with her so that the incident becomes a true learning experience. It is important, however, that work be completed prior to the debriefing if at all possible.

This is only one example of the difficulties in cases involving both giftedness and other learning or behavioral difficulties. The strategies mentioned throughout the book can be utilized in these and other scenarios to improve student outcome and reduce the frustrations for both the teacher and the student.

We've gone through several of the more typical situations that come up in the area of internal and external behavior, as well as risky situations. In each of the scenarios, most of the communication by the parents was appropriate. However, none of the initial dialogues concentrated on understanding what the behavior was communicating. This is one of the biggest differences when the parent takes on the role of emotional coach for her child—a shift from managing behavior to understanding and shaping the way in which the child reacts with his world.

There are numerous other scenarios I could have included in this book. But these provide an initial framework from which you can model your own unique situations. The important thing to remember is that using the principle of good coaching can change difficult and potentially explosive situations into ones that help mold and shape child behavior, resulting in improvements over time. With the use of these strategies, parents and teachers can show children how to monitor their own behaviors and adjust them as needed.

FINAL THOUGHTS

Raising gifted children is a difficult job. More often than not, we feel overwhelmed—both because of the intensity we are confronted with every day and our own guilt when we are unsuccessful in our dealings with our children. At those times, it is important to remember that this is a hard job.

Let me say that again—parenting and teaching gifted children is a very hard job.

The strategies I've given you throughout the book will help. But they take time to master. And even with perfect execution of the coaching techniques and behavior strategies, your child will still be intense and may still be very difficult to manage at times.

I say this not to scare you, but remind you that the crazy chaotic times will happen. They are part of life. But they also are powerful teaching moments—moments when you can test out the strategies given, tailor them to your own unique way of parenting, and help your child learn to master his own emotions.

When you struggle, when you feel like you have failed ... remember, there is no way you can fail at this if you are continuously trying to help your child move in the direction of mastery and acceptance of his emotional intensity.

As this happens, as your child becomes more adept and managing his or her emotions, you will see amazing moments—times when your child talks himself out of a negative spin—without your help. Or times when he turns to you as a coach to help him navigate through his situation without yelling at you when you try to help. These are the times when you will see the fruits of your labors.

These are the times to cherish and celebrate—times you can build on to create even more successes. Use those precious moments to get you through the more difficult ones.

I remember, distinctly, the first time my oldest daughter could talk herself out of her temper tantrum. It is a moment that has more meaning for me than almost anything in her childhood.

There is no such thing as perfect parenting, only being the best you can at the moment.

Take the time to learn your own hot-button issues. Know what makes you react emotionally. Understand your own aspects of giftedness. These things will help you become the best parent you can be during the more difficult times.

I love hearing how these strategies have worked for you. Please feel free to contact me with your own stories and suggestions at christine@ christinefonseca.com. Together we can improve the lives of all gifted children and help them recognize the full impact of their gifts—the passion for life that is their intensity.

RECOMMENDED RESOURCES
GENERAL INFORMATION ON GIFTEDNESS

Information related to giftedness can sometimes be hard to find. Fortunately there are a few fantastic websites that provide information on every topic imaginable as it relates to giftedness, advocating for the gifted, and the most recent research in the field. Here are a few of my favorite and most trusted websites.

✦ **National Association for Gifted Children—http://www.nagc.org**
A great site for everything from advocacy efforts to the latest research in the field.

✦ **Supporting the Emotional Needs of the Gifted—http://www.sengifted.org**
Great articles related to the social and emotional needs of gifted children. Also, a great source for information related to forming parent support groups.

✦ **Davidson Institute for Talent Development—http://www.davidsongifted.org**
An excellent site for articles related to giftedness.

Other resources related to general information on giftedness can be found in the next section.

GENERAL PARENTING RESOURCES

Parenting gifted children can pose unique challenges. Some of the best resources for a more in-depth look at general parenting strategies that work well with gifted children include the following books.

✦ *A Parent's Guide to Gifted Children* by James T. Webb, **Janet L. Gore, Edward R. Amend, and Arlene R. DeVries (Great Potential Press, 2007)**
  A comprehensive parenting book that covers the characteristics of giftedness, emotional intensity, and good parenting techniques.

✦ *Parenting Gifted Kids: Tips for Raising Happy and Successful Children* by James R. Delisle (Prufrock Press, 2006)
  A good overview of gifted children and parenting strategies.

✦ *Keys to Parenting the Gifted Child* (3rd ed.) by Sylvia Rimm **(Great Potential Press, 2007)**
  A good basic overview of the characteristics of giftedness and parenting strategies.

✦ *Raising a Gifted Child: A Parenting Success Handbook* by **Carol Fertig (Prufrock Press, 2008)**
  This book contains a wealth of resources parents of children already identified as gifted can use to help supplement their children's educations.

WORKING WITH INTENSE BEHAVIORS

Dealing with emotional intensity is exhausting work. Understanding why gifted children are as intense as they are can help make the work of parenting them much easier. For more information on emotional intensity try these resources.

✦ *Living With Intensity: Understanding the Sensitivity, Excitability, and the Emotional Development of Gifted Children, Adolescents, and Adults* edited by Susan Daniels and Michael Piechowski (Great Potential Press, 2008)
This book provides an excellent basis in Dabrowski's theories for those wishing to have more information in this area.

✦ *Smart Teens' Guide to Living With Intensity: How to Get More Out of Life and Learning* by Lisa Rivero (Great Potential Press, 2010)
This is a nice book for teens with additional strategies for living an intense life.

✦ Kazimierz Dabrowski's Theory of Positive Disintegration site—http://www.positivedisintegration.com
This site provides detailed information on Dabrowski's theories.

FORMING PARENT GROUPS

Parent groups can be a rich source of support and information for parents both in traditional and nontraditional learning environments. The following are my two favorite resources for those interested in forming your own group.

✦ Supporting Emotional Needs of the Gifted—
http://www.sengifted.org
Great source of information for finding or starting a parent
support group.

✦ *Gifted Parent Groups: The SENG Model* (2nd ed.) by Arlene
R. Devries and James T. Webb (Great Potential Press,
2007)
A comprehensive resource for parent groups based on the
SENG model.

SPECIFIC TOPICS

I covered a large array of topics in the role-play and strategies sections of the book. For further reading on some of the bigger topics, I have provided a list of my favorite resources. Not all of these books deal directly with gifted children, but the information and strategies they present are very helpful.

ANXIETY/DEPRESSION

Gifted children are uniquely prone to feelings of anxiety and depression. Some resources when dealing with these types of difficulties include the following.

✦ *Anxiety-Free Kids: An Interactive Guide for Parents and
Children* by Bonnie Zucker (Prufrock Press, 2009)
This is a terrific, interactive guide for children and parents
dealing with anxiety.

✦ *The Anxiety Cure for Kids: A Guide for Parents* by Elizabeth
DuPont Spencer, Robert L. DuPont, and Caroline M.
DuPont (Wiley, 2003)
A great resource for parents dealing with significantly

anxious children. Although the book is geared toward those children diagnosed with anxiety disorders, the strategies will work with less severe cases or cases that are related more to giftedness than an anxiety disorder.

PERFECTIONISM

When I talk with parents about giftedness, the conversation always turns to perfectionism. The following books and sites contain helpful information for parents and children in learning to manage the adverse effects of perfectionism.

✦ *When Gifted Kids Don't Have All the Answers: How to Meet Their Social and Emotional Needs* by Jim Delisle and Judy Galbraith (Free Spirit, 2002)
  A good book geared for children and the problems they tend to face in the educational setting.

✦ *What to Do When Good Enough Isn't Good Enough: The Real Deal on Perfectionism: A Guide for Kids* by Thomas S. Greenspon (Free Spirit, 2007)
  A good resource for younger children, providing lots of practical strategies.

✦ Letting Go of Perfect: Overcoming Perfectionism in Kids by Jill L. Adelson and Hope E. Wilson (Prufrock Press, 2009)
  A comprehensive guide for parents and teachers on the types of perfectionists and specific strategies to work with each type.

BULLYING

Bullying is difficult enough for any child to live with. But when the child in question is gifted, the intensity of his reaction can be unbearable. The following books have helped me become more educated with regard to bullying and ways to help those who are bullied.

✦ *The Bully, the Bullied, and the Bystander: From Preschool to High School—How Parents and Teachers Can Help Break the Cycle* by **Barbara Coloroso (Harper, 2009)**
An outstanding explanation of the bullying triangle, with practical strategies to end the cycle of violence.

✦ *Girl Wars: 12 Strategies That Will End Female Bullying* by **Cheryl Dellasega and Charisse Nixon (Fireside, 2003)**
An excellent resource for relational aggression and other forms for female bullying.

ANGER MANAGEMENT/ CONFLICT RESOLUTION

Sometimes a child's intensity causes conflicts with others. When this conflict gets out of control, strategies related to conflict resolution and anger management can be very helpful. Here is one of my favorite resources when working on these issues.

✦ *Calming the Family Storm: Anger Management for Moms, Dads, and All the Kids* by **Gary D. McKay and Steven A. Maybell (Impact Publishers, 2004)**
An excellent book full of practical strategies for anger management for all members of the household.

Dually Exceptional Children

Dually exceptional children often are misunderstood, even within gifted circles. For more in-depth reading in this area, here are a few of my favorite resources.

✦ *Misdiagnosis and Dual Diagnoses of Gifted Children and Adults: ADHD, Bipolar, OCD, Asperger's, Depression, and Other Disorders* by James T. Webb, Edward R. Amend, Nadia E. Webb, Jean Goerss, Paul Beljan, and F. Richard Olenchak (Great Potential Press, 2005)
This is a great resource for parents, educators, and mental health professionals in understanding the difficulties of properly diagnosing gifted children with dual exceptionalities.

✦ *The Mislabeled Child: How Understanding Your Child's Unique Learning Style Can Open the Door to Success* by Brock Eide and Fernette Eide (Hyperion, 2006)
Another great book explaining how the needs of gifted children can be lost in the sea of labels present in most educational systems.

✦ *Smart Kids With Learning Difficulties: Overcoming Obstacles and Realizing Potential* by Rich Weinfeld, Linda Barnes-Robinson, Sue Jeweler, and Betty Roffman Shevitz (Prufrock Press, 2006)
This book guides parents and teachers in identifying, working with, and building effective programming for gifted children with learning disabilities.

TALKING ABOUT THE BIG STUFF

Most parents shy away from talking with their children about the big stuff—sex, drugs, and alcohol. But when armed with good information, these conversation don't have to be so hard, even with our intense gifted children.

✦   *Staying Connected to Your Teenager: How to Keep Them Talking to You and How to Hear What They're Really Saying* **by Michael Riera (Da Capo Press, 2003)**
A great book to help parents stay connected to the ever-changing world of their teens

✦   *7 Things Your Teenager Won't Tell You: And How to Talk to Them Anyway* **by Jenifer Marshall Lippincott and Robin M. Deutsch (Ballantine Books, 2005)**
A book full of the "hard things" and how to talk to your kids about them.

REFERENCES

Cook, M. (1999). *Effective coaching.* New York, NY: McGraw Hill.

Kulik, J. A. (2004). Meta-analytic studies of acceleration. In N. Colangelo, S. G. Assouline, & M. U. M. Gross (Eds.), *A nation deceived, How schools hold back America's brightest students* (Vol. II, pp. 13–22). Iowa City: The University of Iowa, The Connie Belin and Jacqueline N. Blank International Center for Gifted Education and Talent Development.

Lind, S. (2001). Overexcitability and the gifted. *The SENG Newsletter, 1*(1), 3–6. Retrieved from http://www.sengifted.org/articles_social/Lind_OverexcitabilityAndTheGifted.shtml

Mueller, C. (2009). Protective factors as barriers to depression in gifted and nongifted adolescents. *Gifted Child Quarterly, 53,* 3–14.

Pipher, M. (1994). *Reviving Ophelia: Saving the selves of adolescent girls.* New York, NY: Ballantine.

Reis, S. M., & Hébert, T. P. (2008). Gender and giftedness. In S. I. Pfeiffer (Ed.), *Handbook of giftedness in children: Psychoeducational theory, research, and best practices* (pp. 271–291). New York, NY: Springer.

Renzulli, J. S., & Park, S. (2000). Gifted dropouts: The who and the why. *Gifted Child Quarterly, 44,* 261–271.

Silverman, L. K. (1989). Invisible gifts, invisible handicaps. *Roeper Review, 12,* 27–42.

Swiatek, M. A., & Lupkowski-Shoplik, A. (2000). Gender differences in academic attitudes among gifted elementary school students. *Journal for the Education of the Gifted, 23,* 360–377.

Sword, L. (2006a). *Parenting emotionally intense gifted children.* Retrieved from http://talentdevelop.com/articles/ParentingEIGC.html

Sword, L. (2006b). *Psycho-social needs: Understanding the emotional, intellectual and social uniqueness of growing up gifted.* Retrieved from http://talentdevelop.com/articles/PsychosocNeeds.html

Sword, L. (2006c). *The gifted introvert.* Retrieved from http://talentdevelop.com/articles/GiftIntrov.html

Treffinger, D. J. (1982). Demythologizing gifted education: An editorial essay. *Gifted Child Quarterly, 26,* 3–8.

Treffinger, D. J. (2009). Guest editorial. *Gifted Child Quarterly, 53,* 229–232.

Webb, J. T. (2008, August). *Dabrowski's theory and existential depression in gifted children and adults.* Presentation at The Eighth International Congress of the Institute of Positive Disintegration in Human Development, Calgary, Alberta, Canada. Retrieved from http://www.sengifted.org/articles_counseling/DabrowskisTheory.pdf.

Webb, J. T., Amend, E. R., Webb, N. E., Goerss, J., Beljan, P., & Olenchak, F. R. (2005). *Misdiagnosis and dual diagnoses of gifted children and adults: ADHD, bipolar, OCD, Asperger's, depression, and other disorders.* Scottsdale, AZ: Great Potential Press.

Webb, J. T., Gore, J. L., Amend, E. R., & DeVries, A. R. (2007). *A parent's guide to gifted children.* Scottsdale, AZ: Great Potential Press.

ABOUT THE AUTHOR

Christine Fonseca has worked in the field of education for more than 10 years. Relying on her expertise as a school psychologist, she has been a resource to parents and educators for understanding the social and emotional needs of gifted children. She holds a master's degree in school psychology and has served as a school psychologist, speaker, consultant, parenting coach, and trainer. Currently, Christine conducts trainings for parents and educators in the Southern California area, where she lives with her husband and precocious gifted daughters. In addition to writing books related to giftedness, Christine writes novels for teens and adults. When she is not directly working with children and parents, she spends her time at her favorite coffeehouse writing her next book. If you would like to learn more about Christine, please visit: http://www.christinefonseca.com.